superfoods

First published in 2014 by Bauer Media Books, Australia
Reprinted in 2014, 2015 (twice), 2016.
Bauer Media Books are published by
Bauer Media Pty Limited

BAUER MEDIA BOOKS
Publisher Jo Runciman
Editorial & food director Pamela Clark
Director of sales, marketing & rights Brian Cearnes
Creative director & designer Hieu Chi Nguyen
Senior editor Stephanie Kistner
Food concept director & food editor Sophia Young
Writer Dr Joanna McMillan
Operations manager David Scotto
Published by Bauer Media Books,
a division of Bauer Media Pty Limited,
54 Park St, Sydney; GPO Box 4088, Sydney, NSW 2001.
phone (02) 9282 8618; fax (02) 9126 3702
www.awwcookbooks.com.au

Printed by Leo Paper Products in China.
Title: Superfoods.
ISBN: 978-1-74245-473-3 (paperback)
Notes: Includes index.
Subjects: Cooking (Natural foods). Natural foods. Cooking (Cereals). Nutrition.
Other Authors/Contributors: Clark, Pamela.
Dewey Number: 641.5637

© Bauer Media Pty Limited 2014
ABN 18 053 273 546
This publication is copyright. No part of it may be reproduced or transmitted in any form without the written permission of the publishers.

Photographer Ben Dearnley
Stylist Michelle Noerianto
Photochef Dominic Smith

Recipe developers Olivia Andrews, Cynthia Black, Charlotte Binns-McDonald, Angela Devlin, Alexandra Elliott, Jane Howard

Cover (front) Miso almond vegie patties, page 42; Labne and tomato salad with seeds, page 32:
Cover (back) Spelt crêpes with poached pear and blueberries, page 225.

To order books
phone 136 116 (within Australia) or
order online at www.awwcookbooks.com.au
Send recipe enquiries to:
recipeenquiries@bauer-media.com.au

contents

superfood by Dr Joanna McMillan	6
dairy & eggs	8
grains, pulses & nuts	34
versatile vegies	76
super seafood	136
lean meats	174
fruit & chocolate	210
glossary	234
conversion chart	237
index	238

superfood

While there are many controversies in the world of nutrition, the one thing no one argues about is that the foods we choose to eat have an enormous impact on our health and wellbeing. Diet is implicated in pretty much every chronic disease that ails us including the big three – heart disease, cancer and type 2 diabetes. But diet also affects the way we look, the way we feel and our ability to perform at our best during work and play. We instinctively know this, and the fact that you have picked up this book is testament to your endeavours towards ensuring you make the best food choices.

Enter the realm of 'superfoods'. It does seem as if there is a new one touted every week, often on the back of some gorgeous celebrity who names it as one of their secrets to health and vitality. Often the prized superfood is expensive and hard to get hold of, at least until the wise producers get hold of it and ramp up distribution. Just think of how many 'superfood' berries, flown from the Amazon or other exotic locations, or a grain or seed consumed by ancient populations such as the Aztecs or Incas, has become the latest must-have food in the savvy, health-conscious consumer's shopping basket. All this hype over foods has to make us question what makes a food a 'superfood' and are they all they are cracked up to be?

making superfood status

The truth is, there is no official criteria for establishing superfood status. It's a word that has become commonplace in describing foods with something special about them. Usually they are foods that have exceptionally high antioxidant power, or have some unique beneficial plant chemical that we can't find elsewhere. Perhaps the food is an especially good source of one or more vitamins or minerals, or is terrifically rich in fibre. In essence, while the definition of a superfood is discretionary, these are foods that have some special nutritional attribute to offer us.

our choice of superfoods

The great news is that superfoods are not all exotic products flown half way around the world. Most of the superfoods we have selected in this book are everyday foods that you will find in your local supermarket or grocer. This is purposeful. While some of these more exotic foods may well have benefits, equally there are many fabulous foods that are produced here in Australia with proven nutritional benefits that warrant superfood status.

select a powerful team

While there are many superfoods, not one of them has the power to make much of a difference to your health on its own. It is the team of foods that make up your diet that ultimately counts. The more different fresh healthy foods you have in your diet, the more you diversify your intake of nutrients and beneficial compounds. There are many different healthy diets but what they all have in common is that they are based on wholesome, natural, minimally processed foods. This book is intended to inspire you to use the most nutritious of those foods to create a mouth-watering menu for you and your family. It's delicious eating, that just happens to be good for you too.

Dr Joanna McMillan
Accredited Practising Dietitian and Nutritionist
www.drjoanna.com.au
www.getlean.com.au

dairy & eggs

Perhaps not the most likely superfoods, we uncover how protein-rich dairy and eggs can help you to control your weight and boost your health.

This Middle Eastern dish contains protein-rich ingredients: eggs, yoghurt and, the seed and nut mixture, dukkah. If you eat this for breakfast, it will help to keep your blood sugar levels in check for the rest of the day. And this means you are less likely to succumb to quick-fix snacks.

fried eggs and spiced yoghurt sauce

2 tablespoons olive oil

1 clove garlic, crushed

½ teaspoon dried mint

½ teaspoon sweet paprika

1 teaspoon cumin seeds

cooking oil spray

4 free-range eggs

½ cup (140g) Greek-style yoghurt, warmed

1 tablespoon dukkah

2 tablespoons loosely packed fresh mint leaves

2 wholemeal pitta breads (170g), char-grilled

1 Heat oil in a 22cm (9-inch) frying pan (base measurement) over medium heat; cook garlic, dried mint and spices, stirring for 1 minute or until fragrant. Spoon into a bowl; set aside.
2 Wipe out pan with paper towel. Lightly spray pan with cooking oil. Heat pan over medium heat; cook eggs for 4 minutes or until whites are set and yolks remain runny. Add yoghurt to pan; remove from heat.
3 Sprinkle eggs with dukkah and mint leaves; drizzle with spiced oil. Season to taste. Serve with pitta bread.

prep + cook time 15 minutes **serves** 2
nutritional count per serving 38.6g total fat (9.6g saturated fat); 2802kJ (670 cal); 51.6g carbohydrate; 25.7g protein; 7g fibre

tips Warm yoghurt in the microwave oven for 20-30 seconds. Char-grill pitta bread in a heated grill pan or on a barbecue grill plate.

The secret to successful poached eggs is to use fresh eggs. As an egg ages, the white breaks down becoming runny and so doesn't cling to the yolk as well. Check the cartons when you buy eggs and select one with the longest use-by-date.

poached eggs, flat mushrooms and spinach with kumara rösti

1 medium lemon (140g)

1 fresh long red chilli, seeded, chopped finely

2 tablespoons chopped fresh lemon thyme

1 clove garlic, crushed

½ cup (125ml) extra virgin olive oil

4 flat mushrooms (480g), stems removed

2 small kumara (orange sweet potato) (600g), grated coarsely

1 tablespoon wholemeal plain (all-purpose) flour

5 free-range eggs

1 tablespoon white vinegar

¼ cup (60ml) olive oil

600g (1¼ pounds) english spinach, trimmed

1 Preheat oven to 180°C/350°F.
2 Remove rind from lemon with a zester, into long thin strips. Squeeze juice from lemon; you will need 2½ tablespoons juice.
3 Stir rind, chilli, lemon thyme, garlic and extra virgin olive oil in a small saucepan over low heat for 5 minutes or until mixture is warm. Remove from heat; stir in juice. Season.
4 Place mushrooms on an oven tray. Drizzle with some of the lemon chilli dressing; season. Bake for 15 minutes or until mushrooms are tender.
5 Meanwhile, squeeze excess moisture from grated kumara. Combine kumara, flour and 1 egg in a medium bowl; season. Heat half the olive oil in a large frying pan over medium heat. Add a quarter of the kumara mixture, flatten with a spatula to form a 13cm (5¼-inches) round; cook for 2 minutes each side or until browned and cooked through. Transfer to a tray; cover with foil to keep warm. Repeat with remaining mixture to make four rösti in total, adding more olive oil to pan when necessary.
6 To poach eggs, half-fill a large deep frying pan with water, add vinegar; bring to a gentle simmer. Break 1 egg into a cup. Using a wooden spoon, make a whirlpool in the water; slide egg into whirlpool. Repeat with a second egg. Cook eggs 3 minutes or until whites are set and yolks remain runny. Remove eggs with a slotted spoon; drain on a paper-towel-lined plate. Keep warm. Repeat poaching with remaining eggs.
7 Heat remaining olive oil in a large saucepan over medium-high heat, add spinach; cook, covered, stirring occasionally, for 2 minutes or until just wilted. Season.
8 Divide rösti among plates; top with spinach, mushrooms and eggs. Drizzle eggs with remaining lemon chilli dressing.

prep + cook time 40 minutes **serves** 4
nutritional count per serving 49.5g total fat (8.7g saturated fat); 2757kJ (615 cal); 23g carbohydrate; 17g protein; 7g fibre

tip If you don't have a zester, you can finely grate the lemon rind instead.

lime and cardamom sheep's milk yoghurt with tropical fruit

2 medium limes
½ medium red papaya (525g), peeled, seeded
1 small ripe pineapple (350g), trimmed, peeled, halved lengthways, cored
2 small bananas (260g), quartered lengthways
1 cup (280g) sheep's or goat's milk yoghurt
¼ teaspoon ground cardamom
2 tablespoons oat bran
⅓ cup (55g) blanched almonds, roasted, sliced coarsely
1½ tablespoons honey

1 Remove rind from 1 lime with a zester, into long thin strips. Finely grate rind from remaining lime. Squeeze juice from limes; you will need ¼ cup juice.
2 Cut fruit into wedge shapes. Place fruit in a large bowl with grated rind and juice; toss gently to combine.
3 Combine yoghurt and cardamom in a small bowl.
4 Spoon fruit mixture into bowls; top with half the oat bran, then the yoghurt mixture. Sprinkle with remaining oat bran, then nuts and lime strips. Drizzle with honey.

prep time 20 minutes **serves** 4
nutritional count per serving 11g total fat (2.4g saturated fat); 1174kJ (280 cal); 33g carbohydrate; 8.8g protein; 6g fibre

Kidney beans are a great source of protein, complex carbohydrates, minerals and several vitamins. However, they do lack the full spectrum of essential amino acids – serve the frittata with a slice of wholegrain bread or scatter it with sesame seeds to get them all.

kidney bean, onion and rocket frittatas with avocado dressing

3 medium red onions (450g)

250g (8 ounces) cherry truss tomatoes, cut into four clusters

2½ tablespoons olive oil

1 teaspoon ground cumin

8 free-range eggs, beaten lightly

½ cup (125ml) buttermilk

1 cup (45g) chopped rocket (arugula) leaves

400g (12½ ounces) canned red kidney beans, drained, rinsed

1 ripe medium avocado (250g)

3 teaspoons lime juice

½ cup (140g) natural yoghurt

2 tablespoons chopped fresh coriander (cilantro)

2 tablespoons chopped fresh flat-leaf parsley

10g (½ ounce) rocket (arugula) leaves, extra

1 Preheat oven to 180°C/350°F.
2 Cut each onion into four thick slices. Place onion and tomatoes, in a single layer, on a large oven tray. Brush all over with 1 tablespoon of the oil; sprinkle with cumin, then season. Bake for 15 minutes or until tomatoes have softened. Remove tomatoes; cover with foil to keep warm. Bake onions a further 5 minutes or until golden and tender.
3 Combine egg, buttermilk and chopped rocket in a medium bowl; season. Oil four 14cm (5½-inch) ovenproof mini frying pans with remaining oil; divide onion slices and beans among pans. Heat pans over medium heat, add a quarter of the egg mixture to each pan; cook for 2 minutes or until mixture is half set. Transfer pans to oven; bake for 13 minutes or until just set.
4 Meanwhile, mash avocado in a medium bowl; stir in juice, yoghurt and herbs. Season to taste.
5 Turn frittatas out onto serving plates; top with tomatoes, extra rocket and a spoonful of avocado dressing.

prep + cook time 1 hour **serves** 4
nutritional count per serving 34g total fat (8.5g saturated fat); 2089kJ (499 cal); 19.6g carbohydrate; 24.4g protein; 9g fibre

tip You can also make the frittata in a 21cm (8½-inch) frying pan (base measurement), however you will need to cook the egg mixture in step 3 for 5 minutes or until half set, then bake it for 15 minutes or until set.

If you buy yoghurt with live cultures (probiotic bacteria) these have the potential to boost the growth of beneficial bacteria in your gut while minimising the growth of pathogenic bacteria. The knock-on benefits to your health include a stronger immune system with fewer coughs and colds, and a healthier gut.

DAIRY FOODS can also help to reduce blood pressure and big population studies show associations with lower risk of type 2 diabetes.

BUT OF COURSE not all yoghurts are the same. They have different levels of fat, added sugars, may have fruit and other additions, and some are thickened with gums or have other additives. Our advice is to always read the ingredients list to know exactly what you are getting. Your absolute best options are natural yoghurts with live cultures, and nothing else in the ingredients list.

yoghurt

Yoghurt is simply fermented milk and it probably came about as a method of making milk last longer. In doing so there were unexpected side effects and they were beneficial. Many cultures (excuse the pun) around the world from Nepal and India to the Middle East and Europe have long considered yoghurt a medicinal food and for good reason.

While many people cut out dairy foods from their diet while trying to lose weight, this is quite contradictory to what the research shows. Studies where dairy foods are included as part of an energy restricted diet show that they promote better weight loss, and most importantly they seem to help improve body composition.

That means they help you to lose fat and keep your muscle – exactly what you want for a lean and fit body. Just what it is about dairy that is responsible for this effect is not fully understood, but it seems to be a combination of the protein, the amino acid leucine and the calcium that are all found in dairy products.

THE LIVE BACTERIA in the yoghurt also helps to break down the milk carbohydrate, lactose. This means that if you are lactose intolerant, as many adults are, you might well find that while you are running to the loo after milk, you can eat yoghurt. That's a bonus, as yoghurt is rich in top-quality protein, is an excellent source of calcium and gives you a serious boost in several B group vitamins including riboflavin, magnesium and zinc.

Mushrooms provide B vitamins and essential minerals; leafy asian greens provide vitamin C, beta-carotene and potassium, and few kilojoules. Ginger and chilli are no slouches nutritionally either, both contain powerful antioxidants.

soft-boiled egg and brown rice nasi goreng

400g (12½ ounces) gai lan

375g (12 ounces) choy sum

½ cup firmly packed fresh coriander (cilantro) leaves

4 free-range eggs

2 tablespoons peanut oil

6 shallots (150g), halved, sliced thinly

4cm (1½-inch) piece fresh ginger (20g), cut into thin matchsticks

2 cloves garlic, crushed

2 fresh long red chillies, sliced thinly

150g (4½ ounces) button mushrooms, quartered

100g (3 ounces) shiitake mushrooms, sliced thinly

115g (3½ ounces) baby corn, halved lengthways

3½ cups (625g) cooked brown rice

1 teaspoon sesame oil

2 tablespoons kecap manis

1 Cut stalks from gai lan and choy sum. Cut stalks into 10cm (4-inch) lengths; cut leaves into 10cm (4-inch) pieces. Keep stalks and leaves separated. Chop half the coriander; reserve remaining leaves.
2 Cook eggs in a medium saucepan of boiling water for 5 minutes or until soft-boiled; drain. When cool enough to handle, peel eggs.
3 Meanwhile, heat half the peanut oil in a wok over medium heat; stir-fry shallots for 8 minutes or until soft and light golden. Add ginger, garlic and half the chilli; stir-fry for 4 minutes or until softened. Transfer mixture to a plate.
4 Heat remaining peanut oil in wok over medium-high heat; stir-fry mushrooms and corn for 4 minutes or until just tender. Add asian green stalks; stir-fry 3 minutes. Add asian green leaves, rice, sesame oil, kecap manis, shallot mixture and chopped coriander; stir-fry 3 minutes or until rice is hot and leaves are wilted. Season to taste.
5 Serve nasi goreng topped with reserved coriander leaves, remaining chilli and eggs.

prep + cook time 45 minutes **serves** 4
nutritional count per serving 18.2g total fat (3.8g saturated fat); 2206kJ (527 cal); 61g carbohydrate; 22.8g protein; 13g fibre

tip You will need to cook 1½ cups (300g) brown rice for the amount of cooked rice needed in this recipe.

baked ricotta with char-grilled vegetables and salsa verde

cooking oil spray

750g (1½ pounds) firm ricotta

1 free-range egg

¼ cup (20g) finely grated parmesan

¼ cup chopped fresh chives

¼ teaspoon dried chilli flakes

5 fresh bay leaves

1 medium eggplant (440g), cut lengthways into 5mm (¼-inch) slices

2 medium red capsicums (bell peppers) (400g), cut into eight thick slices

2 medium zucchini (240g), sliced thinly lengthways

12 slices wholegrain sourdough bread (135g)

salsa verde

1¾ cups lightly packed fresh basil leaves

2 cups lightly packed fresh flat-leaf parsley leaves

2 cloves garlic, crushed

2 anchovy fillets, chopped

2 teaspoons baby capers

1 teaspoon finely grated lemon rind

⅓ cup (80ml) extra virgin olive oil

2 teaspoons lemon juice

1 Preheat oven to 180°C/350°F. Spray an 18cm (7¼-inch) springform pan with cooking oil spray; line base and side with baking paper.
2 Combine ricotta, egg, parmesan and chives in a large bowl; season. Spoon mixture into pan, level surface; sprinkle with chilli flakes and press bay leaves on top. Bake for 35 minutes or until puffed and centre is firm. Stand in pan for 5 minutes before transferring to a platter.
3 Meanwhile, make salsa verde.
4 Spray vegetables and bread slices with cooking oil spray; season. Cook vegetables on a grill plate (grill or barbecue) over medium-high heat for 2 minutes each side or until charred and tender. Char-grill bread for 1 minute each side or until lightly charred.
5 Serve baked ricotta with vegetables, bread and salsa verde.
salsa verde Process herbs, garlic, anchovy, capers, rind and half the oil until coarsely chopped. With motor operating, add remaining oil in a thin stream, processing until mixture is smooth. Transfer mixture to a small bowl, stir in juice; season to taste. Cover surface with plastic wrap.

prep + cook time 1 hour 15 minutes **serves** 6
nutritional count per serving 30g total fat (12g saturated fat); 1776kJ (424 cal); 14.5g carbohydrate; 21.3g protein; 7.4g fibre

Make sure you use a more nutritious wholegrain bread than wholemeal, which is often high GI, or multigrain, which can simply be white bread disguised with a smattering of seeds and grains.

french toast with poached cherries

4 free-range eggs

⅓ cup (80ml) milk

1½ tablespoons coconut oil

8 x 2.5cm (1-inch) thick slices wholegrain bread (300g)

⅓ cup (95g) Greek-style yoghurt

poached cherries

1 vanilla bean

2 medium oranges (480g)

½ cup (125ml) water

¼ cup (60ml) maple syrup

300g (9½ ounces) cherries

1 Make poached cherries.
2 Meanwhile, preheat oven to 120°C/250°F. Place a large wire rack over an oven tray.
3 Lightly whisk eggs and reserved vanilla seeds (from poached cherries) in a medium bowl until combined; whisk in milk.
4 Heat half the coconut oil in a large frying pan over medium heat until melted. Dip four bread slices, one at a time, into egg mixture, turning until soaked; drain away excess. Cook bread in pan for 2 minutes each side or until browned and firm to touch in the centre. Transfer to a wire rack; keep warm in oven.
5 Repeat step 4 with remaining oil, bread and egg mixture.
6 Serve toast with poached cherries and yoghurt.
poached cherries Split vanilla bean lengthways; scrape out seeds. Reserve seeds for french toast. Thinly peel a strip of rind from one orange. Squeeze juice from oranges; you will need ½ cup juice. Combine vanilla bean, rind, juice, the water and syrup in a small saucepan; bring to a simmer. Add cherries; simmer, uncovered, for 3 minutes. Remove from heat; stand cherries in syrup for 10 minutes.

prep + cook time 30 minutes **serves** 4
nutritional count per serving 17.8g total fat (10g saturated fat); 1953kJ (470 cal); 57.5g carbohydrate; 16.3g protein; 6.4g fibre

tips You can use any type of milk you prefer – almond, rice, soy, goat's and cow's milk are all suitable. If you don't have coconut oil use olive oil instead. Use a gluten-free bread for a coeliac-friendly version of this recipe.

Lutein and zeaxanthin have been associated with a reduced risk of age-related macular degeneration and cataracts.

Protein Rich

Eggs provide very high quality protein, with a near perfect balance of the amino acids the human body needs. There's a reason why eggs have been a body-builders' staple for many years. Scientific research is unequivocal in support of higher protein diets for weight control, and eggs are a terrific food to boost the protein content of a meal.

EGG NUTRITION

A SERVE OF 2 LARGE EGGS PROVIDES 580KJ, 12.7G OF PROTEIN, 10.3G OF FAT AND 1.4G OF CARBOHYDRATE. OF THE FAT, LESS THAN A THIRD IS SATURATED FAT AND OVER HALF IS HEALTHY MONOUNSATURATED FAT – THE SAME FAMILY OF FAT FOUND IN OLIVE OIL AND AVOCADO. IMPORTANTLY EGGS ARE A TERRIFIC SOURCE OF THE LONG CHAIN OMEGA-3 FATS ESSENTIAL TO OUR HEALTH. THESE FATS ARE ALL FOUND IN THE YOLK, ALONG WITH A WEALTH OF VITAMINS, MINERALS AND ANTIOXIDANTS. SO DON'T THROW THE YOLK AWAY.

The egg yolk is also rich in several essential minerals and trace elements including iodine (often low in our diets and necessary for correct thyroid function), iron, selenium (with an important antioxidant role) and smaller amounts of zinc and magnesium.

eggs

If you're confused over eggs you're not alone. Once upon a time, before we really understood how diet affects blood cholesterol levels, it made sense to limit foods high in cholesterol. Since egg yolks come under that category, the advice was to limit the number of eggs you ate. Today we know that the types of fat in your diet plays a more important role in determining your blood cholesterol profile and dietary cholesterol is far less of a factor. Even if you have high blood cholesterol, you can happily enjoy up to 6 eggs a week.

The yolk is especially rich in the B group vitamins folate, vitamin B5, vitamin B12, thiamin (B1) and riboflavin (B2). The fat is important as it also contains excellent levels of the fat-soluble vitamins A and E, and significant amounts of vitamin D, along with two carotenoids essential for eye health – lutein and zeaxanthin.

Helps Control Your Appetite

Studies have shown that people who eat eggs for breakfast are less hungry later and correspondingly eat less at lunch.

When you look at the entire nutritional profile, eggs are hard to beat.

huevos rancheros

1 tablespoon extra virgin olive oil

1 medium onion (150g), chopped

250g (8 ounces) mini red capsicums (bell peppers), quartered

2 cloves garlic, crushed

2 teaspoons ground cumin

1kg (2 pounds) ripe vine-ripened tomatoes, chopped coarsely

400g (12½ ounces) canned red kidney beans, drained, rinsed

2 tablespoons coarsely chopped fresh coriander (cilantro) leaves

100g (3 ounces) drained persian fetta, crumbled

4 free-range eggs

1 fresh green jalapeño chilli, sliced thinly

⅓ cup loosely packed fresh coriander (cilantro) sprigs, extra

1 Heat oil in a large frying pan over medium heat; cook onion and capsicum, stirring, for 5 minutes or until soft. Add garlic and cumin; cook, stirring, until fragrant. Stir in tomatoes and beans; simmer, uncovered, 20 minutes or until sauce thickens. Season to taste. Stir in coriander.
2 Meanwhile, preheat oven to 180°C/350°F; place a 1 litre (4-cup) ovenproof dish in the oven while preheating.
3 Pour hot tomato mixture into hot dish, top with fetta; make four indents in the mixture. Break eggs into a cup, one at a time, sliding each into an indent. Sprinkle with chilli. Bake for 8 minutes or until whites of eggs are set and egg yolks are just beginning to set. (The cooking time will vary depending on what your ovenproof dish is made from, and may take up to 15 minutes to cook.)
4 Serve topped with extra coriander.

prep + cook time 45 minutes **serves** 4
nutritional count per serving 16.7g total fat (6.2g saturated fat); 1356kJ (324 cal); 19.3g carbohydrate; 19.6g protein; 9.5g fibre

tips The tomato mixture can be made a day ahead; reheat before adding the eggs. If you can't find mini capsicums, use 1 medium-sized capsicum instead and cut into chunky pieces.

serving suggestion Serve with wholegrain tortillas.

It's hard to eat poorly when you've got a carton of eggs in the fridge, even if there's little else around. Eggs represent very compact packets of protein and nutrients ready to be turned into a nutritious meal in minutes. Master an omelette then you can create a filling according to what you have on hand.

mushroom, tomato and goat's cheese omelettes

1 tablespoon extra virgin olive oil

400g (12½ ounces) mixed mushrooms, sliced (such as button, swiss brown, flat, enoki, shimeji)

1 clove garlic, crushed

½ teaspoon chopped fresh thyme leaves

200g (6½ ounces) grape tomatoes, halved

8 free-range eggs

⅓ cup (80ml) water

100g (3 ounces) drained marinated goat's cheese

1 Heat half the oil in a 20cm (8-inch) frying pan over medium-high heat; cook mushrooms, stirring occasionally, for 8 minutes or until browned.
2 Add garlic, thyme and tomatoes; cook, stirring, for 2 minutes or until tomatoes are just softened. Season to taste. Remove from pan; cover to keep warm. Wipe pan clean.
3 Lightly beat eggs and the water with a pinch of salt in a large bowl until combined.
4 Heat ½ teaspoon of the remaining oil in same pan over high heat. Add a quarter of the egg mixture, tilting the pan so it covers the base. Draw the outside edge of the egg mixture into the centre of the pan with a lifter or spatula, letting the uncooked egg run over the base. Repeat until egg is almost set. Top half the omelette with a quarter each of the mushroom mixture and cheese. Fold omelette over; slide out of pan onto a plate, folding in half again as it slides onto the plate.
5 Repeat step 4 with remaining oil, egg mixture, mushroom mixture and cheese. If you like, serve omelettes topped with extra thyme sprigs and freshly ground black pepper.

prep + cook time 25 minutes **serves** 4
nutritional count per serving 20.7g total fat (7.4g saturated fat); 1204kJ (287 cal); 3g carbohydrate; 21.5g protein; 2.4g fibre

tip Omelettes are best served immediately, but can be kept warm in a 150°C/300°F oven for a few minutes while cooking the remaining omelettes.

Labne is yoghurt that has been drained of whey. A short draining time will result in a thick creamy yoghurt; a longer draining time, like this recipe, will achieve the consistency of a soft cheese, that can be rolled into balls. You will need to make the labne a day ahead.

labne and tomato salad with seeds

You will need to start this recipe the day before.

2 teaspoons sesame seeds

2 teaspoons sunflower seeds

2 tablespoons coarsely chopped pistachios

2 teaspoons ground cumin

1 teaspoon sea salt flakes

400g (12½ ounces) baby heirloom tomatoes

250g (8 ounces) truss cherry tomatoes

200g (6½ ounces) yellow grape tomatoes

200g (6½ ounces) red grape tomatoes

½ cup (60g) sicilian green olives

½ small red onion (50g), sliced thinly

3 cups (350g) firmly packed watercress sprigs

¼ cup loosely packed fresh coriander (cilantro) sprigs

labne

1 teaspoon sea salt flakes

500g (1 pound) Greek-style yoghurt

dressing

¼ cup (60ml) extra virgin olive oil

1½ tablespoons lemon juice

1 clove garlic, quartered

1 Make labne and dressing.
2 Dry-fry seeds, nuts, cumin and salt in a medium frying pan, stirring, over low heat for 5 minutes or until fragrant. Cool.
3 Halve or thickly slice some of the larger tomatoes; place all tomatoes in a large bowl. Slice cheeks from olives close to the pits; discard pits. Add olives, onion, watercress, coriander and half the dressing to the bowl; toss gently to combine. Season to taste.
4 Serve tomato salad topped with labne and seed mixture; drizzle with remaining dressing.

labne Stir salt into yoghurt in a small bowl. Line a sieve with two layers of muslin or a clean chux cloth; place sieve over a deep bowl or jug. Spoon yoghurt mixture into sieve, gather cloth and tie into a ball with kitchen string. Refrigerate 24 hours or until thick, gently squeezing occasionally to encourage the liquid to drain. Discard liquid. Roll or shape tablespoons of labne into balls.

dressing Place ingredients in a screw-top jar, season to taste; shake well. Stand at least 20 minutes or refrigerate overnight. Discard garlic before using.

prep time 35 minutes (+ refrigeration) **serves** 4
nutritional count per serving 28.5g total fat (7.8g saturated fat); 1863kJ (445 cal); 29.2g carbohydrate; 13.5g protein; 7.6g fibre

tips You will need 1 large bunch of watercress for this recipe. Labne can be made 5 days ahead. Refrigerate labne, covered with olive oil, in a small shallow container. Drain before using. You can use 150g (4½ ounces) crumbled fetta or soft goat's cheese instead of labne.

serving suggestion Serve with wholemeal turkish or afghan bread.

grains, pulses & nuts

Diets rich in grains, pulses and nuts are among the healthiest in the world, adding years to life and life to years.

The flavours of warming spices, sour/sweet pomegranate, salty cheese and tangy yoghurt all dance happily together in this salad with nutty quinoa. For something different, swap the quinoa for either lentils, freekeh or barley.

quinoa salad with haloumi and pomegranate

1 cup (200g) red or white quinoa

2 cups (500ml) water

1 clove garlic, crushed

2 tablespoons lemon juice

2 teaspoons ground cumin

2 teaspoons ground coriander

¼ cup (60ml) olive oil

½ cup loosely packed fresh mint leaves

100g (3 ounces) baby spinach leaves

½ cup (75g) sunflower seeds, toasted

250g (8 ounces) haloumi, cut into 1cm (½-inch) slices

¾ cup (210g) Greek-style yoghurt

⅓ cup (50g) pomegranate seeds

1 Bring quinoa and the water to the boil in a medium saucepan; cook, covered, over low heat for 15 minutes or until tender. Drain; cool slightly.
2 Combine garlic, juice, spices and 1 tablespoon of the oil in a large bowl; season to taste. Add quinoa to bowl with mint, spinach leaves and seeds; toss gently to combine.
3 Heat remaining oil in a large frying pan over high heat; cook haloumi for 1 minute each side or until golden.
4 Serve quinoa salad topped with haloumi, yoghurt and pomegranate seeds.

prep + cook time 25 minutes **serves** 4 as a light lunch
nutritional count per serving 40.6g total fat (12g saturated fat); 2792kJ (667 cal); 43.5g carbohydrate; 48.3g protein; 7g fibre

tips Fresh pomegranate seeds can sometimes be found in the fridge section of supermarkets or good green grocers. If unavailable, cut a whole pomegranate in half and scrape the seeds from flesh with your fingers while holding the pomegranate upside down in a bowl of cold water; the seeds will sink and the white pith will float. Make sure you cook the haloumi just before serving, as it becomes tough and rubbery on cooling.

Our take on the traditional Italian salad panzanella, includes cannellini beans and cheese beefing up the nutritional content with protein making it more of a main than a side salad. If you like, skip the cheese and stir through a can of flaked drained tuna.

spicy white bean panzanella

- 160g (5 ounces) wholegrain sourdough bread
- cooking oil spray
- 1 medium lemon (140g)
- 800g (1½ pounds) canned cannellini beans, drained, rinsed
- 250g (8 ounces) heirloom cherry tomatoes, halved
- 2 lebanese cucumbers (260g), chopped
- 1 small red onion (100g), sliced thinly
- ½ cup (60g) pitted sicilian olives, halved
- 1 fresh long red chilli, sliced thinly
- 1 cup loosely packed fresh basil leaves, torn
- 120g (4 ounces) soft goat's cheese, crumbled
- ¼ cup (60ml) olive oil
- ⅓ cup (80ml) red wine vinegar
- 1 clove garlic, crushed

1 Preheat oven to 220°C/425°F. Line a large oven tray with baking paper.
2 Roughly tear bread into pieces, place on tray; spray with cooking oil. Bake 5 minutes or until golden and crisp.
3 Remove rind from lemon with a zester, into long thin strips.
4 Place bread in a large bowl with rind, beans, tomatoes, cucumber, onion, olives, chilli, basil and half the cheese; toss gently to combine.
5 Combine oil, vinegar and garlic in a small bowl; season to taste. Spoon dressing over salad; top with remaining cheese. Serve immediately.

prep + cook time 20 minutes **serves** 4
nutritional count per serving 23g total fat (6g saturated fat); 1825kJ (436 cal); 32g carbohydrate; 18.3g protein; 12g fibre

tips If you don't have a zester, you can finely grate the lemon rind instead. You can use marinated fetta instead of goat's cheese, if you like.

pulses

If you've previously thought of pulses as the fare of vegetarians, it's time to reconsider. Pulses include chickpeas, lentils and dried beans such as borlotti, cannellini, red kidney, turtle beans and black-eyed peas. These pack a pretty powerful nutritional punch, being rich in plant protein, providing slow release, low GI carbohydrates, stacks of fibre and a wealth of vitamins, minerals and beneficial plant chemicals.

The carbohydrates

in pulses are very slowly absorbed, giving pulses very low glycaemic index values. For example chickpeas have a GI of 36, and lentils vary according to kind but are in the range 21-42 (low GI foods are those with a score less than or equal to 55). This makes them very good at filling you up and keeping hunger at bay for longer. The knock-on effect is that you eat less and weight control is easier. The lower GI also means your body doesn't need to produce as much insulin as with higher GI foods. This makes it easier for your body to burn fat, control blood glucose levels and in the long run, reduce your risk of diabetes.

PULSES

ARE PACKED WITH FIBRE AND NOT JUST ANY OLD FIBRE. WE NOW KNOW THAT PARTICULAR TYPES OF FIBRES PLAY DIFFERENT ROLES AND THE NEW KID ON THE BLOCK, RESISTANT STARCH, SEEMS TO BE ESPECIALLY IMPORTANT FOR GUT HEALTH. THE FRIENDLY BACTERIA LIVING IN YOUR COLON THRIVE ON RESISTANT STARCH AND IT IS THE PRODUCT OF THIS FERMENTATION PROCESS THAT BOOSTS OUR GUT HEALTH AND OVERALL IMMUNE FUNCTION.

There are several characteristics that might be contributing to these amazing effects of pulses. Firstly replacing some animal protein with the plant proteins in pulses, tends to improve blood cholesterol profiles.

Eating more pulses might also help you to live longer. A study of older people from varying dietary cultures including Australia, Japan, Sweden and Greece, found that intake of pulses was the strongest dietary predictor of survival. Who knew that such a humble food group could have such a powerful effect on health? In fact for every additional 20g of pulses consumed, the risk of death was 7-8 percent lower.

Pulses are high-ranking players when it comes to beneficial plant compounds. They contain a wealth of phytochemicals that have been shown to benefit our health including phytosterols, isoflavones, saponins, alkaloids and phytates.

While phytates have received some bad press mostly on account of their ability to bind minerals such as iron, lowering their absorption, overall phytates have been associated with beneficial effects. By consuming a varied diet with plenty of foods rich in minerals, you needn't worry about the small amounts that may be caught up with phytates.

miso almond vegie patties

2 tablespoons white (shiro) miso

2 tablespoons sesame seeds, roasted

1 cup (160g) almonds, roasted

2 tablespoons vegetable oil

2 green onions (scallions), chopped

180g (5½ ounces) swiss brown mushrooms, chopped coarsely

1 tablespoon light soy sauce

1 teaspoon chinese five-spice powder

2 teaspoons honey

½ cup (35g) panko (japanese) breadcrumbs

1 free-range egg, beaten lightly

2 tablespoons vegetable oil, extra

½ cup (150g) whole-egg mayonnaise

2 teaspoons lime juice

1 lime, cut into wedges

pickled cabbage salad

450g (14½ ounces) red cabbage, shredded finely

2 green onions (scallions), sliced thinly

4 radishes (140g), sliced thinly

1 tablespoon chopped pickled ginger

2 tablespoons lime juice

2 tablespoons rice wine vinegar

1 tablespoon light soy sauce

1 teaspoon caster (superfine) sugar

1 Make pickled cabbage salad.
2 Process miso, seeds and nuts until roughly combined; leave mixture in processor.
3 Heat oil in a large frying pan over medium heat; cook onion and mushrooms for 3 minutes or until browned. Add sauce and five spice; cook for 30 seconds. Add mushroom mixture to processor with honey, breadcrumbs and egg; pulse until well combined but not smooth. Shape 1½ tablespoons of the mixture into 12 patties.
4 Heat half the extra oil in a large frying pan over medium heat; cook patties, in three batches, 2 minutes each side or until golden, adding remaining oil in between batches.
5 Combine mayonnaise and juice in a small bowl.
6 Serve patties with pickled cabbage salad, lime mayonnaise and lime wedges.

pickled cabbage salad Place cabbage, onion, radish and ginger in a large bowl. Pour combined juice, vinegar, sauce and sugar over salad; toss gently to combine.

prep + cook time 30 minutes **serves** 4
nutritional count per serving 59.2g total fat (6.2g saturated fat); 3079kJ (736 cal); 27g carbohydrate; 19.4g protein; 10.6g fibre

tip You can form the mixture into four burger patties then serve with mayonnaise and cabbage salad in wholemeal buns.

rosemary and tomato barley risotto with mozzarella

1 tablespoon olive oil

1 small onion (80g), chopped finely

2 cloves garlic, crushed

1 medium red capsicum (bell pepper) (200g), sliced

1 tablespoon fresh rosemary, chopped finely

1½ cups (300g) pearl barley

1.25 litres (5 cups) vegetable stock

400g (12½ ounces) canned diced tomatoes

1 cup (280g) bottled tomato passata

2 teaspoons caster (superfine) sugar

2 teaspoons finely grated lemon rind

200g (6½ ounces) buffalo mozzarella, torn

1 tablespoon chilli-infused olive oil

½ cup loosely packed fresh flat-leaf parsley leaves

1 Heat olive oil in a large saucepan over medium heat; cook onion, garlic, capsicum and rosemary for 5 minutes or until tender.
2 Add barley; cook, stirring, for 1 minute. Add stock, tomatoes, passata, sugar and rind; bring to the boil. Reduce heat to low; cook, stirring occasionally, for 45 minutes or until barley is tender. Season to taste.
3 Spoon risotto into bowls; top with mozzarella, drizzle with chilli oil and sprinkle with parsley.

prep + cook time 55 minutes **serves** 4
nutritional count per serving 24.5g total fat (9.2g saturated fat); 2476kJ (592 cal); 61.6g carbohydrate; 24.8g protein; 13.7g fibre

tips You could also use large balls of fresh cow's milk mozzarella, which are known as fior di latte – literally meaning 'flower of the milk'. Use a pinch of chilli flakes or a little chopped fresh chilli and extra virgin olive oil instead of the chilli-infused oil. Passata is pureed and sieved Italian tomatoes and is available from supermarkets.

spiced chickpea and cauliflower dosa

2 tablespoons vegetable oil

1 large onion (200g), chopped finely

2 cloves garlic, crushed

2 teaspoons cumin seeds

4cm (1½-inch) piece fresh ginger (20g), grated finely

1 tablespoon indian curry powder

2 teaspoons yellow mustard seeds

500g (1 pound) cauliflower, cut into small florets

400g (12½ ounces) canned chickpeas (garbanzo beans), drained, rinsed

1 cup (250ml) vegetable stock

1½ tablespoons vegetable oil, extra

3 limes, halved

½ cup loosely packed fresh coriander (cilantro) leaves

cucumber yoghurt

1 cup (280g) Greek-style yoghurt

1 lebanese cucumber (130g), grated coarsely

1 teaspoon dried mint

dosa batter

1 cup (150g) chickpea flour (besan)

1 cup (150g) plain (all-purpose) flour

1 teaspoon ground cumin

½ teaspoon bicarbonate of soda (baking soda)

¼ teaspoon sea salt flakes

2 cups (500ml) cold tap water

1 Heat oil in a large frying pan over medium heat; cook onion, garlic, cumin, ginger, curry powder and mustard seeds for 5 minutes or until onion is soft. Add cauliflower and chickpeas; cook stirring, for 2 minutes. Add stock; cook, partially covered, for 15 minutes or until cauliflower is tender. Roughly mash cauliflower and chickpeas with the back of a spoon. Season to taste. Set aside; keep warm.
2 Make cucumber yoghurt.
3 Make dosa batter.
4 Heat 1 teaspoon of the extra oil in a 25cm (10-inch) frying pan over medium heat. Add ½ cup of batter and quickly spread with a metal spatula to cover the base; cook 2 minutes or until mixture bubbles. Top with one-sixth of the cauliflower mixture; cook a further 2 minutes or until base is crisp and golden. Roll up dosa to enclose filling; slide onto a plate. Repeat with remaining oil, batter and cauliflower mixture to make six dosa in total.
5 Serve dosa with cucumber yoghurt and lime halves, scattered with coriander.
cucumber yoghurt Combine ingredients in a medium bowl. Season to taste.
dosa batter Sift flours, cumin, bicarbonate of soda and salt into a bowl. Whisk in the water until combined.

prep + cook time 45 minutes **makes** 6
nutritional count per dosa 17.3g total fat (3.5g saturated fat); 1823kJ (436 cal); 51g carbohydrate; 14.3g protein; 8.2g fibre

tips Chickpea flour (besan) is available from the health food aisle of supermarkets or health food stores. Keep dosa warm in a preheated 180°C/350°F oven in between batches.

Sunflower seeds

are one of the richest sources of vitamin E, with a tablespoon of seeds providing 22% of what experts reckon women need in a day, and 16% for men. Vitamin E is the chief fat-soluble antioxidant in the body, and plays a crucial role in protecting cells from damage, including sun damage to the skin. That's one reason why you'll find vitamin E in so many face creams, but you want to make sure you feed your skin from the inside out too.

Pumpkin seeds are an excellent source of magnesium, needed for more than 300 biochemical reactions in the body. You need it for a healthy immune system, to keep your blood pressure where it should be, for normal muscle and nerve function, to manage blood glucose levels and to keep your bones strong.

FLAXSEED IS ESPECIALLY RICH IN FIBRE. ADDING JUST A TABLESPOON TO YOUR BREAKFAST DELIVERS AN EXTRA 3G OF FIBRE. FLAXSEED, ALONG WITH CHIA, IS A STAND-OUT AMONGST SEEDS AS BEING ONE OF THE HIGHEST SOURCES OF PLANT OMEGA-3 FATS. WHILE THESE ARE NOT QUITE THE SAME AS THE LONG CHAIN OMEGA-3s FOUND IN OILY FISH, THEY ARE BENEFICIAL NONETHELESS AND PLAY AN ANTI-INFLAMMATORY ROLE IN THE BODY.

Quinoa is rich in several B group vitamins required to turn the food you eat into energy to fuel your body. A serve of quinoa will provide you with folate, thiamin, riboflavin, vitamin B6 and smaller amounts of niacin.

seeds & quinoa

Quinoa (pronounced keen-wa) is cooked and eaten as a grain alternative, but it is in fact a seed. You'll often hear it called a pseudo-grain for that reason, similar to amaranth. While it might be relatively new to many of us, quinoa has been a staple food for thousands of years in the Andean region of South America. The Incas reportedly considered it sacred, calling it 'the mother of all grains'.

Seeds are the means by which many plants procreate. The seed must therefore give the new seedling the nutrition it needs to sprout and grow. That's why they are such nutritional powerhouses. They provide good quality protein, providing all of the essential amino acids, making them an especially good addition to a vegetarian meal. You'll find a wealth of antioxidants and other beneficial plant compounds, many unique to seeds.

The oldest living person in the world (at the time of writing) is a 123-year old Bolivian farmer. He attributes his long life, free of any serious illness, to his traditional Andean diet with quinoa as a staple food.

A STUDY OF over 5,000 Finnish adults, followed for 14 years, found that those with higher vitamin E intakes from food were significantly less likely to die from heart disease.

Quinoa earns superfood status as it boasts an impressive nutritional profile. It has double the protein of rice and provides all of the essential amino acids – the building blocks of protein.

indian-spiced quinoa cakes with tomatoes

400g (12½ ounces) kumara (orange sweet potato), peeled, cut into 4cm (1½-inch) cubes

2 cups (500ml) water

1 cup (200g) white quinoa

⅓ cup (80ml) olive oil

1 medium onion (150g), chopped finely

2 cloves garlic, crushed

4cm (1½-inch) piece fresh ginger (20g), grated finely

1 fresh long red chilli, chopped finely

1½ tablespoons indian curry powder

⅓ cup chopped fresh coriander (cilantro)

1 free-range egg

¼ cup (40g) wholemeal plain (all-purpose) flour

1 tablespoon olive oil, extra

500g (1 pound) ripe roma (egg) tomatoes, each cut into 6 wedges

1 tablespoon yellow mustard seeds

2 tablespoons fresh curry leaves

⅔ cup (190g) Greek-style yoghurt

2 cups (40g) baby asian salad leaves

1 Cook kumara in a medium saucepan of boiling water for 5 minutes or until tender. Drain well. Mash kumara; you will need 1 cup. Cool.
2 Bring the water to the boil in a small saucepan. Stir in quinoa; cook, covered, over low heat for 15 minutes or until tender. Drain well. Cool.
3 Heat 1 tablespoon of the oil in a medium frying pan over medium heat; cook onion, stirring, for 8 minutes or until soft. Add garlic, ginger, chilli and curry powder; cook, stirring, over low heat for 3 minutes or until soft and fragrant.
4 Combine mashed kumara, quinoa and onion mixture in a large bowl with coriander, egg and flour; season. Form level ½-cups of mixture into eight 8cm (3¼-inch) patties. Place on a baking-paper-lined tray. Cover; refrigerate for 30 minutes or until chilled.
5 Heat the remaining oil in a large frying pan over medium heat; cook patties, in batches, for 3 minutes each side or until golden and heated through. Drain on paper towel.
6 Heat extra oil in same frying pan over medium heat; cook tomatoes, mustard seeds and curry leaves, stirring occasionally, for 5 minutes or until tomato is softened. Season to taste.
7 Serve quinoa cakes with tomatoes, yoghurt and salad leaves.

prep + cook time 50 minutes (+ cooling & refrigeration)
serves 4
nutritional count per serving 31.4g total fat (6.3g saturated fat); 2556kJ (611 cal); 61.5g carbohydrate; 16g protein; 8.9g fibre

This textural salad of grains, nuts and fruits can be eaten as a light lunch or serve it as a side dish with chicken or lamb. Grapes would make a nice alternative to the cherries.

chickpea, barley, orange and cherry salad

You will need to soak the barley in cold water for 3 hours before you start this recipe. Drain barley before use.

1½ cups (300g) pearl barley

500g (1 pound) butternut pumpkin, cut into 1.5cm (¾-inch) pieces

1 tablespoon olive oil

2 teaspoons cumin seeds

2 medium oranges (480g)

400g (12½ ounces) canned chickpeas (garbanzo beans), drained, rinsed

⅓ cup (55g) almonds, roasted, chopped coarsely

¼ cup (35g) sunflower seeds, toasted lightly

300g (9½ ounces) cherries, halved, pitted

¼ cup chopped fresh mint

2 tablespoons chopped fresh flat-leaf parsley

2 tablespoons pomegranate molasses

½ cup (125ml) extra virgin olive oil

2 tablespoon small fresh mint leaves, extra

1 Preheat oven to 220°C/425°F.
2 Cook soaked barley in a large saucepan of boiling water for 25 minutes or until tender; drain. Rinse under cold water; drain well.
3 Meanwhile, combine pumpkin, olive oil and cumin seeds on a large oven tray; season. Bake for 20 minutes or until tender and beginning to brown around edges.
4 Remove rind from oranges with a zester, into long thin strips. Segment oranges over a bowl to catch the juices (see tip); reserve 2 tablespoons of juice.
5 Place barley, pumpkin, orange segments and rind in a large bowl with chickpeas, nuts, seeds, cherries and herbs. Combine reserved juice, pomegranate molasses and extra virgin olive oil in a small jug. Drizzle dressing over salad, season to taste; toss gently to combine. Serve salad topped with extra mint.

prep + cook time 45 minutes (+ standing) **serves** 4
nutritional count per serving 49.1g total fat (6.7g saturated fat); 3784kJ (904 cal); 87.3g carbohydrate; 19.1g protein; 22.5g fibre

tip To segment oranges: cut top and bottom from oranges with a small sharp knife. Cut remaining rind and white pith from oranges, following the curve of the fruit. Holding the oranges over a bowl, cut down both sides of the white membrane to release each segment. Squeeze membrane to release any juices into the bowl.

seeded pumpkin bread

900g (1¾-pound) butternut pumpkin, halved lengthways, seeds removed

2 teaspoons (7g) dried yeast

1 tablespoon honey

½ cup (125ml) lukewarm water

2 tablespoons vegetable oil

1⅓ cups (200g) wholemeal plain (all-purpose) flour

2 cups (300g) '00' flour, bread flour or plain (all-purpose) flour

½ cup (75g) sunflower seeds

2 tablespoons sesame seeds

1 tablespoon linseeds

1 tablespoon sea salt flakes

1 egg, beaten lightly

2 tablespoons pepitas (pumpkin seeds)

2 teaspoons poppy seeds

1 Preheat oven to 180°C/350°F.
2 Place pumpkin on an oven tray, cover with foil; bake for 1¼ hours or until very tender. When cool enough to handle, scoop flesh into a medium bowl; mash with a fork. You will need 1½ cups mashed pumpkin.
3 Combine yeast, honey and the water in a small bowl; cover with plastic wrap. Stand in a warm place for 10 minutes or until frothy. Stir in oil.
4 Combine flours, seeds and salt in a large bowl. Add yeast mixture and mashed pumpkin; mix to a soft dough. Knead dough on a floured surface for 10 minutes or until smooth and elastic. (If you have an electric mixer with a dough hook, mix on medium speed for 6 minutes or until smooth and elastic.) Place dough in a large oiled bowl; cover with plastic wrap. Stand in a warm place for 1 hour or until doubled in size.
5 Increase oven to 220°C/425°F. Punch down the dough with your fist. Knead on a floured surface 1 minute or until smooth. Shape dough into a 20cm (8-inch) round; place on a large oiled oven tray. Cover loosely with oiled plastic wrap. Stand in a warm place for 40 minutes or until almost doubled in size.
6 Brush dough with egg, sprinkle with pepitas and poppy seeds. Using a sharp, thin-bladed knife, make five shallow cuts across the top of the dough. Bake for 20 minutes. Reduce oven to 180°C/350°F; bake a further 10 minutes or until golden and bread sounds hollow when tapped. Cool on a wire rack.

prep + cook time 2 hours (+ standing) **serves** 8
nutritional count per serving 14.4g total fat (1.6g saturated fat); 1719kJ (411 cal); 53.5g carbohydrate; 12.3g protein; 8.7g fibre

Traditionally harira is a Moroccan soup of lamb, vegetables and pulses, popularly served to break the fast of Ramadan. Our version omits the meat.

vegetable harira soup

You will need to start this recipe the day before.

1 cup (200g) dried chickpeas (garbanzo beans)

large pinch saffron threads

2kg (4 pounds) ripe tomatoes

2 tablespoons olive oil

2 medium onions (340g), chopped coarsely

2 sticks celery (300g), trimmed, chopped coarsely

1½ teaspoons ground cinnamon

1 teaspoon ground turmeric

1 teaspoon ground ginger

1.25 litres (5 cups) water

1 cup (200g) French-style green lentils

½ cup coarsely chopped fresh flat-leaf parsley

½ cup coarsely chopped fresh coriander (cilantro)

1 Soak chickpeas overnight in a medium bowl of cold water. Drain; rinse well.
2 Soak saffron in a small bowl with 1 tablespoon water.
3 Cut a shallow cross in the base of tomatoes; place in a large bowl. Cover with boiling water, stand for 30 seconds; drain. Remove skins and discard; puree flesh in a blender.
4 Heat oil in a large saucepan over medium heat; cook onion, celery, ground spices and saffron with soaking liquid, stirring for 5 minutes or until vegetables have softened. Add pureed tomatoes, the water and chickpeas; bring to the boil. Skim off any scum that rises to the surface. Reduce heat to low; simmer, partially covered, for 45 minutes. Add lentils; simmer, partially covered for 45 minutes or until lentils and chickpeas are tender. Season with salt.
5 Stir half the herbs through soup. Divide soup among bowls; serve topped with remaining herbs.

prep + cook time 2 hours (+ standing) **serves** 6
nutritional count per serving 14.1g total fat (2g saturated fat); 1516kJ (362 cal); 28.4g carbohydrate; 23.4g protein; 17.9g fibre

serving suggestion Serve with bread rolls.

Romesco is a traditional northern Spanish sauce, much like pesto in texture, made from a mixture of nuts and fire-roasted capsicum that often accompanies seafood or a local roasted Catalonian spring onion.

romesco sauce with eggplant and zucchini

olive oil spray

2 medium eggplant (900g), sliced on the diagonal

4 zucchini (480g), sliced thinly, lengthways

⅓ cup (55g) blanched almonds, roasted, chopped coarsely

⅓ cup (45g) skinless roasted hazelnuts, chopped coarsely

¼ cup fresh flat-leaf parsley leaves, torn

romesco sauce

2 medium red capsicum (bell peppers) (400g)

1 medium tomato (150g)

2 tablespoons extra virgin olive oil

2 cloves garlic

2 teaspoons sweet paprika

½ cup (80g) blanched almonds, roasted

½ cup (70g) skinless roasted hazelnuts

2 tablespoons sherry or red wine vinegar

¼ cup (60ml) water

1 Make romesco sauce.

2 Preheat a grill pan to high. Spray vegetables with olive oil; season with salt. Cook vegetables, in batches, for 4 minutes each side until tender and lightly charred.

3 Layer vegetables on a platter; top with nuts and parsley. Serve with romesco sauce.

romesco sauce Roast capsicums and tomato directly over a gas flame on stove-top, turning until charred (or roast in a hot heavy-based frying pan or grill pan, turning, until charred). Wrap individually in foil. Peel away skins. Chop capsicum and tomato; keep separated. Heat half the oil in a medium frying pan over medium heat; cook chopped capsicum and garlic, stirring occasionally, for 3 minutes or until capsicum is soft. Add chopped tomato and paprika; cook for 3 minutes or until tomato softens. Process nuts until finely chopped; add capsicum mixture, sherry and the water, process until smooth. Season to taste.

prep + cook time 35 minutes (+ cooling) **serves** 4
nutritional count per serving 19.4g total fat (0.9g saturated fat); 1135kJ (271 cal); 8.9g carbohydrate; 8.4g protein; 10g fibre

tips Romesco sauce is also delicious with grilled meats and fish. The sauce can be stored in an airtight container in the fridge for up to 1 week.

Brazil nuts are a rich source of the antioxidant mineral selenium. Just 2-3 nuts are all you need to meet your daily requirement.

Pistachios

are different to other nuts in that they contain beta-carotene that can be converted to vitamin A, and lutein. Both vitamin A and lutein are essential for good eye health.

WALNUTS

ARE A STANDOUT FOR PLANT OMEGA-3 FAT ALPHA-LINOLENIC ACID (ALA) WITH 30G OF NUTS PROVIDING 1.9G. ALA CANNOT BE MADE IN THE BODY AND MUST BE OBTAINED FROM OUR DIET. IT SEEMS TO PLAY A ROLE IN HEART HEALTH WITH HARVARD RESEARCHERS RECOMMENDING AN INTAKE OF 2-3G A DAY.

Pecans have an impressively high antioxidant score compared to other nuts. They are especially high in one form of vitamin E called gamma-tocopherols, which help to protect LDL-cholesterol from damage.

nuts

Nuts contain many different nutrients that may account for their beneficial effects on health. They contain low levels of saturated fats and are rich in a variety of unsaturated fats. Pecans, pistachios, almonds, cashews and hazelnuts provide predominately monounsaturated fat – similar to the type of fat in olive oil. Brazil nuts, walnuts and pine nuts are rich in polyunsaturated fats. These fats are known to improve blood cholesterol profiles. Nuts also contain vitamin E, antioxidants, folate, arginine and plant sterols, all of which contribute to heart health.

Cashews

and pine nuts top the nut charts for iron and zinc. Try consuming with a vitamin-C rich piece of fruit to optimize iron intake, especially if you are a vegetarian.

Almonds are head and shoulders above other nuts for vitamin E. A handful is pretty much all you need for your daily vitamin E quota.

With their rich fat content, nuts are relatively energy-dense foods. Once upon a time, before we knew any better, they were therefore restricted foods on any weight loss diet. Fortunately nuts are back on the menu for weight control, with research clearly showing a benefit. Nuts are fibre and protein rich, both factors that slow stomach emptying and have the effect of helping you to feel full and keep hunger pangs at bay.

Eating a healthy breakfast with a good mix of slow-release carbs and protein will help to keep your blood sugar levels in check for the rest of the day. You can skip the poached pear part of this recipe if you like and top with a mix of fresh or frozen berries instead.

muesli with poached pears and sheep's milk yoghurt

⅓ cup (95g) almond butter
⅓ cup (80ml) pure maple syrup
2 cups (180g) rolled oats
1 cup (50g) flaked coconut
½ cup (80g) flaked almonds
¼ cup (50g) pepitas (pumpkin seeds)
¼ cup (35g) sunflower seeds
¼ cup (20g) quinoa flakes
¼ cup (35g) rolled amaranth or rolled rye
2 tablespoons black or white chia seeds
1 cup (160g) dried sweetened cranberries
6 small corella pears (600g)
2 cups (500ml) apple juice
2 cups (500ml) water
1½ cups (420g) sheep's milk yoghurt

1 Preheat oven to 160°C/325°F. Line a large roasting pan with baking paper.
2 Stir almond butter and maple syrup in a small saucepan over low heat just until combined.
3 Combine oats, coconut, nuts, pepitas, seeds, quinoa and amaranth in a large bowl. Pour syrup mixture over dry ingredients; working quickly, stir to coat ingredients.
4 Spread muesli, in an even layer, in pan. Bake for 15 minutes. Remove from oven; stir well. Bake a further 5 minutes or until oats are golden. Cool for 10 minutes; stir in chia seeds and cranberries.
5 Meanwhile, peel, halve and core pears, leaving stalks intact. Place pears in a medium saucepan with juice and the water; bring to the boil. Reduce heat; cover pears with a round of baking paper, simmer 8 minutes or until tender.
6 Serve muesli topped with yoghurt and poached pears. If you like, drizzle with honey.

prep + cook time 45 minutes **serves** 6
nutritional count per serving 36.8g total fat (9g saturated fat); 2862kJ (684 cal); 61g carbohydrate; 19g protein; 16g fibre

tips Similarly to quinoa, amaranth is treated as a grain. You will be able to find the ingredients for this muesli either in the health food aisle at most supermarkets or health food stores. The muesli will keep in an airtight container for up to 1 month.

Freekeh is roasted green wheat that contains more nutrients than the mature version of the same grain. It has a delicious nutty taste and texture and is available from major supermarkets and health food stores.

spiced freekeh with cucumber and garlic minted yoghurt

2 tablespoons olive oil

1 large onion (200g), chopped finely

2 cloves garlic, crushed

2 medium carrots (240g), diced

1 teaspoon ground allspice

1 teaspoon ground coriander

½ teaspoon chilli powder

2 teaspoons cumin seeds

1½ cups (300g) cracked greenwheat freekeh

1 bay leaf

2½ cups (625ml) vegetable stock or water

2 small lebanese cucumbers (260g)

1 fresh long green chilli, sliced thinly

½ cup fresh coriander (cilantro) leaves

½ cup (80g) flaked almonds, roasted

garlic minted yoghurt

1½ cups (420g) Greek-style yoghurt

2 garlic cloves, crushed

¼ cup finely chopped fresh mint

1 Heat oil in a large saucepan over medium heat; cook onion, garlic and carrot, stirring, for 3 minutes. Add spices and seeds; cook, stirring, for 2 minutes. Stir in freekeh to coat. Add bay leaf and stock; bring to the boil. Reduce heat to low; cook, covered, for 20 minutes or until most of the liquid is absorbed. Remove from heat; stand, covered, for 10 minutes.
2 Meanwhile, make garlic minted yoghurt.
3 Using a vegetable peeler, peel cucumbers lengthways into long thin ribbons.
4 Serve freekeh mixture topped with yoghurt and cucumber; top with combined chilli, coriander and nuts.
garlic minted yoghurt Combine ingredients in a bowl; season to taste.

prep + cook time 45 minutes **serves** 6
nutritional count per serving 19.4g total fat (4.3g saturated fat); 1886kJ (450 cal); 52g carbohydrate; 14.9g protein; 12.9g fibre

tip You can use 1 teaspoon ground cinnamon instead of the allspice, if you like.

spelt pizza with kumara, pepitas and goat's cheese

2 teaspoons (7g) dried yeast

½ teaspoon salt

2 cups (320g) plain (all-purpose) spelt flour

1 cup (250ml) warm water

⅓ cup (80ml) olive oil

3 medium onions (600g), halved, sliced thinly

2 cloves garlic, crushed

800g (1½ pounds) kumara (orange sweet potato), sliced thinly

⅓ cup (65g) pepitas (pumpkin seeds)

1 fresh long green chilli, seeded, chopped finely

200g (7 ounces) soft goat's cheese, crumbled

20g (¾ ounce) baby rocket (arugula)

1 Combine yeast, salt and flour in a large bowl; make a well in the centre. Stir in the water and 2 tablespoons of the oil until mixed well. Knead dough on a floured surface for 5 minutes until smooth and elastic. Place dough in an oiled bowl; cover with plastic wrap. Stand for 30 minutes or until doubled in size.
2 Heat remaining oil in a large frying pan over medium-high heat; cook onion and garlic, stirring occasionally, for 5 minutes. Reduce heat to low; cook, stirring occasionally, for 20 minutes or until onion is light golden. Cool.
3 Preheat oven to 220°C/425°F. Oil two 30cm (12-inch) pizza trays.
4 Divide dough in half, roll each half to a 25cm (10-inch) round; place on tray. Spread onion mixture between pizza bases; top with kumara, slightly overlapping the slices, and pepitas.
5 Bake pizzas for 15 minutes, swapping trays halfway through cooking time, or until crust is golden. Serve topped with chilli, cheese and rocket.

prep + cook time 1 hour 20 minutes (+ standing) **serves** 4
nutritional count per serving 37.5g total fat (11g saturated fat); 3517kJ (840 cal); 91g carbohydrate; 29.4g protein; 18.5g fibre

tips Use a mandoline or V-slicer to easily cut the kumara into thin slices. For extra protein, add 2 tablespoons chia seeds to the pizza dough.

grains, pulses & nuts

Raw capsicums are often hard to digest. Long, slow cooking softens the texture and tempers the taste, accentuating their sweetness and making them easier to digest.

spelt pasta with braised capsicum, nuts and chilli

¼ cup (60ml) olive oil

1 medium onion (150g), chopped finely

2 cloves garlic, crushed

1 teaspoon fennel seeds

3 medium red capsicums (bell peppers) (600g), diced

3 medium yellow capsicums (bell peppers) (600g), diced

1 fresh long red chilli, seeded, chopped finely

2 tablespoons tomato paste

1¾ cups (430ml) vegetable stock

2 tablespoons red wine vinegar

375g (12 ounces) spelt fettuccine

1 cup fresh basil leaves

2 tablespoons pine nuts, toasted

½ cup (40g) shaved parmesan

1 Heat oil in a large saucepan over medium-high heat; cook onion, garlic and fennel seeds, stirring for 5 minutes. Add capsicum and chilli; cook, covered, stirring occasionally, for 8 minutes. Stir in tomato paste; cook for 2 minutes. Add stock; bring to the boil. Reduce heat; simmer, covered, for 25 minutes or until capsicum is very tender. Remove from heat; stir in vinegar. Season to taste.
2 Meanwhile, cook pasta in a large saucepan of salted water until almost tender; drain. Return pasta to the pan.
3 Add capsicum mixture to pasta with half the basil; toss to combine. Serve pasta in bowls topped with pine nuts, cheese and remaining basil.

prep + cook time 50 minutes **serves** 4
nutritional count per serving 23.5g total fat (4.4g saturated fat); 2714kJ (648 cal); 81.4g carbohydrate; 24.6g protein; 9.5g fibre

Labne is yoghurt that has been drained of whey. A short draining time, results in a thick, creamy yoghurt, while a longer one, will achieve the consistency of a soft yoghurt-cheese, that can be rolled into balls. You can make your own (see the recipe on page 32) or buy it from supermarkets.

mediterranean grain salad with honey cumin labne

¾ cup (150g) brown rice

½ cup (100g) French-style green lentils

½ cup (100g) red or white quinoa

1 cup (250ml) water

1 small red onion (100g), chopped finely

2 tablespoons pepitas (pumpkin seeds), toasted

2 tablespoons sunflower seeds, toasted

2 tablespoons pine nuts, toasted

2 tablespoons baby salted capers, rinsed

½ cup (80g) currants

1 cup firmly packed fresh flat-leaf parsley leaves

1 cup firmly packed fresh coriander (cilantro) leaves

¼ cup (60ml) lemon juice

⅓ cup (80ml) olive oil

1 teaspoon cumin seeds, toasted

1 cup (280g) labne

1½ tablespoons honey

½ cup (40g) flaked almonds, roasted

1 Cook rice and lentils, separately, in large saucepans of boiling water for 25 minutes or until tender; drain, rinse well.
2 Place quinoa in a small saucepan with the water; bring to the boil. Reduce heat to low; simmer, covered, for 10 minutes or until tender. Drain.
3 Combine rice, lentils and quinoa in a large bowl. Add onion, seeds, pine nuts, capers, currants, herbs, juice and oil; stir until well combined.
4 Stir cumin seeds into labne in a small bowl.
5 Serve salad on plates or a large platter; top with spoonfuls of labne, drizzle with honey and scatter with almonds.

prep + cook time 1 hour **serves** 6
nutritional count per serving 28.7g total fat (4.2g saturated fat); 2325kJ (555 cal); 56g carbohydrate; 15.5g protein; 8.2g fibre

tip Toast/roast all nuts and seeds together on an oven tray (place the cumin seeds on a small piece of foil to keep them separate), in a 180°C/350°F oven for 8 minutes, stirring halfway through cooking time.

A recent scientific review of 12 large-scale studies found a strong association between intake of whole grains and a 27-30% reduced risk of type 2 diabetes.

Whole grains do not deserve to be thrown into the same nutrition basket as products based on white flour. Big population studies from around the world have consistently shown that eating whole grains is good for us, reducing our risk of chronic diseases including heart disease, diabetes, stroke and certain cancers, and helping us to live longer.

Where we can certainly go wrong is the form in which we eat our grains. Whole grains contain all three parts of the grain kernel – the bran, germ and endosperm. Whereas the process used to make white flour removes the outer layers and only the starchy centre, the endosperm, is used. Unfortunately this process removes a large percentage of the grain nutrients and phytochemicals, along with the fibre. The end result is a refined starch product that inevitably has a high GI.

grains

Grains are staple foods of a majority of diverse cultures around the world, and have been for about 10,000 years. But in today's era of 'carbophobia' grains are often unfairly labelled as 'carbs' and considered fattening. You might be surprised to learn that the breads and cereals' group were the second most important source of protein in the Australian diet in our last nutrition survey. They were also the largest source of fibre, thiamin, magnesium and iron.

FREEKEH (PRONOUNCED FREE-KA) IS AN ANCIENT EASTERN MEDITERRANEAN GRAIN FOOD, MADE FROM ROASTED GREEN WHEAT. BECAUSE THE GRAIN IS HARVESTED WHILE YOUNG IT HAS A FAR HIGHER NUTRIENT CONTENT, INCLUDING MORE PROTEIN, THAN MATURE WHEAT. IT HAS FOUR TIMES THE FIBRE CONTENT OF BROWN RICE AND A LARGE PROPORTION OF THE CARBOHYDRATE PRESENT IS RESISTANT STARCH. THIS MEANS WE CAN'T BREAK IT DOWN AND IT ACTS LIKE A FIBRE, PASSING THROUGH THE GUT TO THE COLON WHERE IT PROMOTES THE GROWTH OF FRIENDLY BACTERIA.

Diversify your intake of whole grains. Choose from barley, brown rice, freekeh, oats, rye or the ancient grains spelt and kamut.

Freekeh is low GI making it ideal for controlling blood glucose levels and weight control, and it's a good source of several nutrients including iron, magnesium, thiamin, copper and zinc.

grains, pulses & nuts

We've left the skin on the pears in this recipe as it has been shown to have twice the fibre of the flesh and a greater concentration of phytonutrients. Any bitterness from the skin and pepperiness from the watercress is easily balanced by the sweetness of the pear flesh.

pasta with almond and walnut paste, pears and broad beans

½ cup (80g) almonds, roasted

½ cup (50g) walnuts, roasted

2 cloves garlic, crushed

¼ cup firmly packed watercress sprigs

½ teaspoon freshly ground black pepper

½ cup (125ml) extra virgin olive oil

400g (12½ ounces) spelt penne pasta

2 medium pears (460g), unpeeled, cored, cut into eight wedges

1 tablespoon olive oil

2 cups (240g) frozen broad (fava) beans, blanched, peeled

1½ cups firmly packed watercress sprigs, extra

⅓ cup (25g) shaved pecorino or parmesan

1 Process nuts, garlic, watercress and pepper until finely chopped. With motor operating, gradually pour in ¼ cup of the extra virgin olive oil until combined. Season with salt to taste.
2 Cook pasta in a large saucepan of boiling salted water for 8 minutes or until almost tender. Drain; reserve ½ cup pasta cooking water. Return pasta to pan; cover to keep warm.
3 Meanwhile, season pears. Heat olive oil in a large frying pan over medium heat; cook pears for 2 minutes each side or until golden. Drain on paper towel.
4 Add nut paste to pasta with enough reserved cooking water, for paste to coat pasta (do not return the pan to the heat or the nut paste will thicken and make the mixture dry). Add pear, broad beans and extra watercress; toss gently to combine. Season to taste.
5 Serve pasta topped with cheese, drizzled with remaining extra virgin olive oil.

prep + cook time 25 minutes **serves** 4
nutritional count per serving 55.7g total fat (7.7g saturated fat); 4182kJ (999 cal); 89.9g carbohydrate; 28.5g protein; 14.2g fibre

tip The nut paste can be made a day ahead; store in an airtight container in the fridge until ready to use.

versatile vegies

Vegies contain a wealth of nutrients and phytochemicals that are essential for optimal health and wellbeing.

Kale, a vegetable rarely featured, is finally in the spotlight. And so it should be. It's a powerhouse of vitamins; tops milk for calcium; and has more iron than meat. Kale has myriad uses cooked or raw.

kale salad with creamy zucchini dressing

1 cup (200g) red or white quinoa

2 cups (500ml) water

200g (6½ ounces) purple kale, trimmed, washed, shredded finely

1 large carrot (180g), unpeeled, grated coarsely

1 cup (100g) walnuts, roasted, chopped coarsely

creamy zucchini dressing

2 small zucchini (180g), chopped coarsely

1 large avocado (320g), chopped coarsely

⅓ cup (35g) walnuts, roasted

1 clove garlic, crushed

2 tablespoons white wine vinegar

2 tablespoons walnut oil

2 tablespoons olive oil

1 Make creamy zucchini dressing.
2 Place quinoa and the water in a medium saucepan; bring to the boil. Reduce heat to low; simmer, covered, for 10 minutes or until tender. Drain; cool.
3 Place quinoa in a large bowl with kale, carrot, nuts and dressing; toss gently to combine. Season to taste.
creamy zucchini dressing Process zucchini, avocado, nuts, garlic and vinegar until smooth. With motor operating, gradually add oils, drop by drop, then in a slow steady stream, until thick and creamy. Season to taste.

prep + cook time 25 minutes **serves** 6
nutritional count per serving 37.8g total fat (4.6g saturated fat); 2041kJ (487 cal); 24.8g carbohydrate; 9.4g protein; 6.6g fibre

tip Quinoa and walnuts are packed with ample protein to make this a meal in itself, however you could serve it as a side dish with grilled chicken, fish or a poached egg. It would also make a delicious filling for wraps or a sandwich.

serving suggestion Serve with grilled chicken breast fillet and lemon wedges.

Pleating the edge of the dumplings can be a little tricky. You can simply press the edges together to ensure they are well sealed – they will be just as tasty.

spinach and ginger dumplings

240g (7½ ounces) english spinach

227g (7 ounces) canned water chestnuts, drained, chopped finely

2 green onions (scallions), chopped finely

4cm (1½-inch) piece fresh ginger (20g), grated finely

1 tablespoon light soy sauce

1 egg, beaten lightly

24 gow gee wrappers (230g)

450g (14½ ounces) firm tofu, sliced thickly

2 tablespoons vegetable oil

2 teaspoons sesame seeds, toasted

½ cup loosely packed fresh coriander (cilantro) leaves

spicy dressing

½ cup (125ml) chinese black vinegar

1 tablespoon lemon juice

1 teaspoon sesame oil

1 fresh small red chilli, sliced thinly

1 Make spicy dressing.
2 Place spinach in a medium heatproof bowl, cover with boiling water; drain immediately. Refresh under cold running water; drain. When cool enough to handle, squeeze excess water from spinach; chop finely.
3 Combine spinach, water chestnuts, onion, ginger, sauce and egg in a bowl. Place 2 teaspoons of the mixture in the centre of a wrapper, leaving a border; brush the edge with water. Fold wrapper over filling; pleat the edge to seal. Repeat with remaining spinach mixture and wrappers.
4 Cook dumplings in a large saucepan of boiling water, in three batches, for 3 minutes or until cooked through. Drain; keep warm.
5 Meanwhile, pat tofu dry with paper towel. Heat oil in a large frying pan over high heat; cook tofu for 2 minutes each side or until golden.
6 Divide tofu and dumplings among bowls; drizzle with dressing, then sprinkle with sesame seeds and coriander.
spicy dressing Combine ingredients in a small bowl.

prep + cook time 30 minutes **serves** 4
nutritional count per serving 23.8g total fat (4g saturated fat); 1939kJ (463 cal); 34g carbohydrate; 21.2g protein; 12g fibre

tip Chinese black vinegar is made from fermented glutinous rice, is mildly acidic and slightly sweet, and is used as a condiment. It is available from Asian food stores (the Chinkiang brand is one of the best). You can use rice vinegar instead.

Superfood greens include spinach, silver beet, kale, cabbage varieties, endive, watercress, and asian greens.

Two of the world's healthiest diets, the Mediterranean diet and the Okinawan diet, have a few common features – one of those is their inclusion of leafy greens.

KALE IS ONE OF THE MOST NUTRITIOUS VEGIES. IT'S PARTICULARLY RICH IN CAROTENOIDS THAT CAN BE CONVERTED TO VITAMIN A IN THE BODY. A SINGLE CUP OF KALE PROVIDES YOU WITH OVER 200% OF YOUR DAILY RECOMMENDED AMOUNT OF VITAMIN A. KALE IS ONE OF THE BEST SOURCES OF THE CAROTENOIDS LUTEIN AND ZEAXANTHIN. THESE ARE KNOWN TO PLAY AN ESSENTIAL ROLE IN EYE HEALTH. A HIGH DIETARY INTAKE IS ASSOCIATED WITH A REDUCED RISK OF AGE-RELATED MACULAR DEGENERATION AND CATARACTS. KALE IS ALSO TERRIFIC FOR VITAMIN C, VITAMIN K, VITAMIN B6, CALCIUM, POTASSIUM, COPPER AND MANGANESE, AND SUPPLIES GOOD LEVELS OF SEVERAL B GROUP VITAMINS INCLUDING FOLATE, IRON, MAGNESIUM AND PHOSPHORUS.

leafy greens

Leafy greens are without doubt one of the top superfoods for you to include in your daily diet. They are among the most nutrient-dense foods, yet contain very few kilojoules and they're anti-inflammatory. That's great news for those of us watching our weight – and that's just about every one of us.

Spinach is one of the most versatile leafy greens and therefore super easy to use to nutrient-boost your day. It contains many of the nutrients found in kale, although in lower amounts for most, but is a better source of folate. Folate is well known for its benefits during early pregnancy, but in fact we all need a decent daily folate hit due to its role in protecting cells and DNA from damage. A high folate intake can slow the ageing process as well as reduce the risk of many chronic diseases. A cup of spinach gives you about 15% of your recommended intake of folate and over half your vitamin A, all for only 30kJ.

Plump out your meal with leafy greens and you achieve volume to help fill you up without the extra kilojoules, truckloads of nutrients and plant chemicals that benefit your health, and you boost your fibre intake to help keep your gut healthy. There are plenty to choose from and generally the darker the leaves the better, but aim for variety. Freshness is key as many nutrients, including vitamin C, will deteriorate with time and exposure to air and light.

versatile vegies 83

Leaving fruit and vegetables unpeeled not only speeds up preparation time, it also makes good nutritonal sense, upping the fibre content of a dish (and in the case of sweet potatoes, the antioxidant content), since the skin contains triple that of the flesh.

roast kumara and pear salad with crunchy chickpeas

400g (12½ ounces) canned chickpeas (garbanzo beans), drained, rinsed

¼ cup (60ml) olive oil

1 tablespoon fennel seeds

2 tablespoons chopped fresh rosemary leaves

650g (1¼ pounds) small kumara (orange sweet potato), unpeeled, cut into wedges

2 medium pears (500g), unpeeled, cut into eight wedges

¼ cup (35g) dried sweetened cranberries

1 cup (250ml) boiling water

1 cup (280g) Greek-style yoghurt

1 tablespoon tahini

200g (6½ ounces) rocket (arugula)

1 Preheat oven to 220°C/425°F.

2 Pat chickpeas dry with paper towel; place on an oven tray. Drizzle 1 tablespoon of the oil over chickpeas, sprinkle with half the fennel seeds and half the rosemary; season. Bake for 20 minutes, stirring occasionally, or until chickpeas are golden and crisp.

3 Reduce oven to 180°C/350°F. Combine kumara and pears on a large oven tray with remaining oil, fennel and rosemary; season. Bake for 40 minutes or until kumara and pears are browned and tender.

4 Meanwhile, soak cranberries in the boiling water for 10 minutes or until softened. Drain, reserving 2 tablespoons of the soaking liquid.

5 Combine yoghurt, tahini and reserved cranberry soaking liquid in a small bowl; season to taste.

6 To serve, arrange rocket, kumara and pears on a large platter; top with chickpeas and cranberries, then drizzle with yoghurt mixture.

prep + cook time 1 hour 15 minutes **serves** 4
nutritional count per serving 23.4g total fat (5.4g saturated fat); 2392kJ (571 cal); 66.1g carbohydrate; 14.6g protein; 13.9g fibre

japanese-style vegetable, tofu and noodle broth

8 dried shiitake mushrooms

1 cup (250ml) boiling water

400g (12½ ounces) small choy sum

200g (6½ ounces) soba noodles

1 tablespoon peanut oil

4 green onions (scallions), sliced thinly

4cm (1½-inch) piece fresh ginger (20g), chopped finely

1.5 litres (6 cups) vegetable stock

¼ cup (60ml) soy sauce

1 teaspoon sesame oil

170g (5½ ounces) asparagus, chopped

200g (6½ ounces) snow peas, chopped

⅔ cup (160g) frozen shelled edamame (soybeans), thawed

300g (9½ ounce) silken tofu, cut into 12 pieces

1 cup (100g) pea tendrils, trimmed

1 Soak mushrooms in the boiling water in a small heatproof bowl for 20 minutes. Drain; reserving soaking liquid. Remove and discard mushroom stems; slice caps.
2 Meanwhile, cut stalks from choy sum. Cut stalks into 10cm (4-inch) lengths; cut leaves into 10cm (4-inch) pieces. Keep stalks and leaves separated.
3 Cook noodles in a large saucepan of boiling water 4 minutes or until just tender. Drain; rinse under cold water, drain well.
4 Heat peanut oil in a large saucepan over medium heat; cook onion and ginger, stirring, for 3 minutes or until soft. Add mushrooms, reserved soaking liquid and stock; bring to the boil. Reduce heat; simmer for 10 minutes.
5 Add sauce, sesame oil, asparagus, snow peas and choy sum stalks; simmer for 2 minutes or until almost tender. Add choy sum leaves and edamame; simmer for 1 minute or until vegetables are tender. Season to taste.
6 Divide noodles and tofu among bowls. Spoon vegetables and broth on top; top with pea tendrils.

prep + cook time 45 minutes **serves** 4
nutritional count per serving 11.8g total fat (2g saturated fat); 1377kJ (329 cal); 26.6g carbohydrate; 25g protein; 12g fibre

tip Pea tendrils, are the tendrils from the vines of a pea plant, they have a mild pea taste and are used in salads and stir-fries. They are available from Asian grocers and specialist green grocers. You can use snow pea shoots instead.

Herbs such as basil, mint and coriander add more than just freshness to our plates. Their leaves are rich in flavonoids and surprisingly high sources of vitamins A and C. Coriander is one of the richest herbal sources of vitamin K.

coconut-roasted pumpkin and cauliflower with chilli, lime and cashews

1 small jap pumpkin (1kg), unpeeled, cut into thick wedges

½ large cauliflower (650g), cut into large florets

2 tablespoons coconut oil, melted

⅓ cup (15g) shaved coconut, roasted

⅓ cup (50g) raw cashews, roasted

¼ cup fresh coriander (cilantro) leaves

¼ cup fresh mint leaves

¼ cup fresh thai basil leaves

dressing

2 teaspoons lime juice

2 tablespoons fish sauce

2 tablespoons brown sugar

2 tablespoons peanut oil

1 fresh long red chilli, chopped finely

2 tablespoons chopped fresh coriander (cilantro)

1 Preheat oven to 220°C/425°F.
2 Place pumpkin and cauliflower on a large oven tray; brush with coconut oil, season. Bake for 30 minutes or until vegetables are brown and tender.
3 Meanwhile, make dressing.
4 To serve, arrange pumpkin and cauliflower on a large platter; drizzle with dressing. Sprinkle with coconut, nuts and herbs.
dressing Combine ingredients in a small jug.

prep + cook time 50 minutes **serves** 4
nutritional count per serving 27.7g total fat (13.2g saturated fat); 1757kJ (420 cal); 28.7g carbohydrate; 9.5g protein; 11.3g fibre

tips Coconut oil is a solidified oil sold in jars and is available from major supermarkets and health food stores. Melt coconut oil as you would butter, either in a small saucepan over low heat or in the microwave. You will need 2 limes for this recipe.

carotenoid vegies

You have no doubt heard of the most famous carotenoid beta-carotene, but in fact there are a whole family of related plant carotenoid compounds, all with their own benefits. Some act as antioxidants, some can be converted to vitamin A in the body and others have specifically been associated with reduced risk of disease.

BETA-CAROTENE CAN BE CONVERTED TO VITAMIN A IN THE BODY AND THIS IS IMPORTANT SINCE VITAMIN A IS NOT SO WIDELY DISTRIBUTED IN FOODS. AN EXCESS OF VITAMIN A CAN ALSO BE TOXIC (IT IS PARTICULARLY HARMFUL DURING PREGNANCY), WHILE THERE IS NO DANGER OF THIS FROM AMPLE BETA-CAROTENE-RICH FOODS. A WORD OF WARNING HOWEVER – SUPPLEMENTS ARE NOT THE SAME. WHILE BETA-CAROTENE RICH DIETS HAVE BEEN SHOWN TO BENEFIT HEALTH, SUPPLEMENTS DO NOT HAVE THE SAME EFFECT AND CAN BE HARMFUL. STICK TO REAL FOODS TO GAIN ALL THE BENEFITS WITHOUT ANY RISKS.

BETA-CAROTENE is what makes carrots (where beta-carotene got its name), sweet potato and pumpkin orange. Many orange coloured fruits including pawpaw and apricots are also sources of beta-carotene. You'll also find high levels of carotenoids in leafy greens such as kale, spinach and cabbage. In these foods the green colour of chlorophyll masks the orange carotenoids, but they are there in abundance.

LYCOPENE is the carotenoid found in tomatoes, but also in red grapefruit, goji berries, guava and papaya. High intakes of lycopene have been associated with a reduced risk of cancer, particularly prostate cancer in men. The amazing thing about lycopene is that it is better absorbed from processed tomatoes than fresh. Tomato paste is a pretty unbeatable source, particularly when teamed with extra virgin olive oil in an Italian style dish. Carotenoids are fat soluble and so a little healthy fat in the recipe boosts your absorption.

LUTEIN & ZEAXANTHIN Two other carotenoids deserve mention – lutein and zeaxanthin. They are found in high concentrations in the eye and seem to play a crucial role in eye development and ongoing eye health throughout life. Those with diets high in these two carotenoids reduce your risk of macular degeneration and from developing cataracts. You'll find them in those dark leafy greens such as kale, spinach and broccoli, as well as in egg yolks.

Broccoli, brussels sprouts and kale are all crucifers – members of the cabbage family, known for its sulphur content, which is dectectable when these vegetables are overcooked. Sulporophane though is a powerful phytochemical that may protect against cancer.

winter vegetable sauté with prosciutto and hazelnuts

300g (9½ ounces) broccoli, cut into florets

300g (9½ ounces) baby brussels sprouts

320g (10 ounces) purple curly kale, trimmed, chopped coarsely

1 medium lemon (140g)

2 tablespoons olive oil

140g (4½ ounces) wholegrain sourdough bread, cut into pieces

75g (2½ ounces) thinly sliced prosciutto, chopped

1 large onion (200g), sliced thinly

4 cloves garlic, sliced thinly

⅓ cup (45g) hazelnuts, roasted, chopped coarsely

½ cup (125ml) chicken stock

1 Cook broccoli in a large saucepan of boiling water for 2 minutes or until just tender but still crisp. Drain immediately; refresh in iced water. Drain well. Repeat with sprouts, then kale.
2 Remove rind from lemon with a zester, into long thin strips (or grate finely). Squeeze juice from lemon; you will need 2 tablespoons juice.
3 Heat half the oil in a large frying pan over medium heat; cook bread pieces, stirring, for 5 minutes or until golden. Remove from pan.
4 Heat remaining oil in same pan over medium heat; cook prosciutto, stirring, for 2 minutes or until crisp. Remove with a slotted spoon; drain on paper towel. Reduce heat to medium-low; cook onion, stirring, for 10 minutes or until very soft. Add garlic; stir for 2 minutes. Add vegetables, rind and nuts; cook, stirring for 5 minutes until combined.
5 Increase heat to high, add stock and juice; simmer 1 minute or until vegetables are tender. Season to taste. Just before serving, scatter with toasted bread.

prep + cook time 45 minutes **serves** 4
nutritional count per serving 20.6g total fat (3g saturated fat); 1519kJ (363 cal); 21.5g carbohydrate; 17.4g protein; 11.3g fibre

While walnuts and other tree nuts are fairly calorific, they offer a veritable array of antioxidant and anti-inflammatory nutrients, as well as valuable monounsaturated and hard-to-source omega-3 fatty acids. If you like, you can use almonds instead of the walnuts in the pesto.

spinach and broccolini pasta with rocket and walnut pesto

400g (12½ ounces) wholemeal spaghetti

470g (15 ounces) broccolini, trimmed, cut into 4cm (1½-inch) lengths

2 tablespoons olive oil

2 cloves garlic, crushed

400g (12½ ounces) baby spinach

1 cup (240g) ricotta, crumbled

½ cup (50g) walnuts, roasted, chopped coarsely

rocket and walnut pesto

60g (2 ounces) rocket (arugula) leaves

1 cup firmly packed fresh basil leaves

½ cup (50g) walnuts, roasted

2 cloves garlic, crushed

1 teaspoon finely grated lemon rind

⅓ cup (25g) finely grated parmesan

½ cup (125ml) extra virgin olive oil

1 Make rocket and walnut pesto.
2 Cook pasta in a large saucepan of boiling salted water for 10 minutes or until almost tender, adding broccolini in last 2 minutes of cooking. Drain well; reserve ½ cup cooking water.
3 Meanwhile, heat oil in a large saucepan over medium heat; cook garlic and spinach, stirring occasionally, for 2 minutes or until just wilted. Season. Add pasta, broccolini, pesto and enough reserved cooking water to help combine the sauce.
4 Serve pasta topped with ricotta and nuts.
rocket and walnut pesto Process rocket, basil, nuts, garlic, rind, cheese and 1 tablespoon of the oil until roughly chopped. With motor operating, add remaining oil in a thin, steady stream until mixture is smooth. Season to taste.

prep + cook time 35 minutes **serves** 6
nutritional count per serving 42.4g total fat (7.8g saturated fat); 2822kJ (674 cal); 49.5g carbohydrate; 20.7g protein; 6.8g fibre

tip It's a good idea to remove the thin paper skins from the walnuts after roasting as they can add a slight bitterness to the pesto. While the nuts are still warm, rub them together in a clean tea towel to remove most of the skins.

wombok and herb salad with beef and tamarind dressing

1 tablespoon vegetable oil

300g (9½ ounces) beef stir-fry strips

½ small wombok (napa cabbage) (350g), shredded finely

1 fresh long red chilli, sliced thinly

¾ cup (105g) roasted peanuts, chopped coarsely

100g (3 ounces) baby spinach leaves

1½ cups fresh mint leaves

½ cup loosely packed fresh vietnamese mint leaves

tamarind dressing

1½ tablespoons tamarind puree

½ cup (175g) brown rice syrup

2 tablespoons lime juice

2 tablespoons fish sauce

1 Make tamarind dressing.
2 Heat oil in a wok over high heat; stir-fry beef for 3 minutes or until cooked through.
3 Place beef in a large bowl with wombok, chilli, peanuts, spinach, herbs and dressing; toss gently to combine.
tamarind dressing Whisk ingredients in a bowl until combined.

prep + cook time 15 minutes **serves** 4
nutritional count per serving 19g total fat (2.6g saturated fat); 1904kJ (455 cal); 41.3g carbohydrate; 28.3g protein; 7g fibre

tips Brown rice syrup is also known as rice syrup or rice malt. It is available in the health food section in most supermarkets. Use prawns, chicken or tofu instead of the beef.

Silver beet is high in non-haeme iron, which is important in a vegetarian diet. Iron from plant sources isn't absorbed as well as haeme iron from meat. Including vitamin C either in the dish (we used lemon juice in this recipe) or with the meal can aid absorption.

silver beet 'risotto'

This recipe is based on the classic Greek leek and rice dish called prasorizo.

- 2 litres (8 cups) water
- 750g (1½ pounds) silver beet (swiss chard)
- 2 tablespoons olive oil
- 2 medium leeks (700g), white part only, sliced thinly
- 2 cloves garlic, crushed
- 1 cup (200g) long-grain or medium-grain brown rice
- ¼ cup (60ml) lemon juice
- ⅓ cup finely chopped fresh dill
- ¼ cup finely chopped fresh flat-leaf parsley
- ⅓ cup (50g) pine nuts, toasted
- 1½ tablespoons extra virgin olive oil
- ⅓ cup (65g) fetta, crumbled
- 1 tablespoon finely grated lemon rind
- 1 medium lemon (140g), cut into wedges

1 Bring the water to the boil in a large saucepan. Reduce heat; keep at a gentle simmer.
2 Cut silver beet stalks from leaves. Trim 2cm (¾-inch) off the end of the stalks; cut stalks into thick slices. Shred silver beet leaves. Keep stalks and leaves separated.
3 Heat olive oil in a large, deep frying pan over medium-high heat; cook silver beet stalks, leeks and garlic, stirring occasionally, for 2 minutes or until just softened. Season. Add rice; cook, stirring, for 1 minute until coated.
4 Stir in 1 cup of the simmering water; cook, stirring over medium-low heat or until liquid is absorbed. Continue adding water, 1-cup at a time, stirring frequently or until water is absorbed after each addition. (You may not need all the liquid if you're using long-grain rice.) Total cooking time should be 45 minutes or until rice is almost al dente. Stir in shredded silver beet leaves; cook a further 5 minutes or until leaves wilt.
5 Remove pan from heat. Stir in juice, herbs and half the pine nuts; season to taste. Spoon mixture into bowls; drizzle with extra virgin olive oil, top with fetta, rind and remaining pine nuts. Serve with lemon wedges.

prep + cook time 1 hour **serves** 4
nutritional count per serving 30.4g total fat (5.8g saturated fat); 2224kJ (531 cal); 45.7g carbohydrate; 13.6g protein; 10.5g fibre

tip You will need about 1 bunch of silver beet for this recipe.

Sichuan is a province in southwest China known for its abundant use of chilli and eye-wateringly fiery dishes. For a milder dish, simply halve the sichuan peppercorns, chillies and chilli flakes in the recipe below.

sichuan gai lan

470g (15 ounces) broccolini

4 green onions (scallions), white and green parts

2 teaspoons sichuan peppercorns

¼ cup (60ml) grape seed oil

1 tablespoon brown rice syrup

4 fresh long red chillies, chopped coarsely

2 teaspoons dried chilli flakes

4 cloves garlic, crushed

400g (12½ ounces) gai lan, cut into thirds

150g (4½ ounces) green beans, trimmed

½ cup (125ml) water

200g (6½ ounces) marinated tofu, sliced

2 tablespoons light soy sauce

1 Cut broccolini in half; keep stems and tops separated. Coarsely chop the white part of the onion; thinly slice the green part. Keep white and green parts separated.
2 Dry-fry peppercorns in a wok over medium heat, stirring continuously, for 2 minutes or until fragrant. Grind peppercorns in a small food processor. Add oil, rice syrup, chilli, chilli flakes, garlic and white part of onion; process until finely chopped.
3 Cook chilli mixture in wok over medium-high heat, stirring, for 3 minutes or until fragrant. Add broccolini stems, gai lan, beans and the water; stir-fry for 1 minute. Add broccolini tops, tofu and sauce; stir-fry for 2 minutes or until tofu is heated through and vegetables are just tender. Serve sprinkled with green part of onion.

prep + cook time 15 minutes **serves** 4
nutritional count per serving 18g total fat (2.7g saturated fat); 1190kJ (284 cal); 9g carbohydrate; 15.6g protein; 13g fibre

tips You will need 2 bunches of broccolini for this recipe. Substitute any of the vegetables in this recipe with another asian green. Tofu can be substituted with barbecued chicken or smoked chicken breast.

Avocado

As well as providing a rich source of healthy monounsaturated fats, avocado is an impressively good source of fibre. Half an avocado contains 6-7g of fibre – almost a quarter of your daily goal. You may also be surprised to know that avocados are a good source of vitamin C. This makes them a great addition to a vegetarian meal as they will help you to absorb more plant iron.

Half an avocado also provides about a fifth of your daily folate needs. Folate protects your DNA and cells all around the body from damage and therefore plays a key role in anti-ageing.

OLIVE OIL

THE MEDITERRANEAN DIET IS HAILED QUITE RIGHTFULLY AS ONE OF THE HEALTHIEST IN THE WORLD. THIS DIET HAS BEEN ASSOCIATED WITH LOWER RATES OF HEART DISEASE, LOWER BLOOD PRESSURE, LOWER RISK OF STROKE, BETTER COGNITIVE HEALTH, LOWER RISK OF DIABETES, AND LOWER RISKS OF MANY CANCERS. THERE ARE MANY FACTORS THAT MAY CONTRIBUTE TO THIS, BUT ONE OF THE KEY CHARACTERISTICS IS THE USE OF OLIVE OIL AS A STAPLE FOOD AND THE PRINCIPAL FAT.

avocado & oil

Remember when we tried to avoid fat of any kind? We now know that eating the right fats is essential for optimal health. Both avocado and olive oil are rich in monounsaturated fats and the only fruits that are fat rich. A solid body of scientific evidence supports making these fats the major ones in your diet. They can help you to achieve a healthier blood cholesterol profile, improve your insulin sensitivity, help you to control blood glucose levels, improve a fatty liver, and even reduce the amount of fat you store around your abdomen. What great news!

It is important to buy extra virgin olive oil however and not products labeled as "light", "pure olive oil" or "pomace". These are all refined products and do not contain the health promoting qualities of fresh extra virgin olive oil. Refining the oil removes many of the antioxidants, phytosterols and polyphenols present in the fresh extra virgin oil that benefit us. Oil is not like wine – it doesn't get better with age. The fresher it is the better. Choose quality over quantity and you will reap the benefits.

It's a myth that cooking with extra virgin olive oil destroys its benefits. Good quality extra virgin olive oil has a high smoke point of around 210 degrees. It can be used for stir-fries, on the BBQ, roasting foods in the oven and pan-frying. Store your oil in a cool dark place to retain the freshness and health-promoting properties. And use it regularly so that you are always consuming this year's batch.

Traditional larb, is a tangy salad of minced pork (or chicken) and fresh herbs, originating from Laos but also found in northern Thailand. This version keeps the traditional flavours and instead mixes them with the crisp textures of raw vegetables.

vegetable larb

2 tablespoons fish sauce

2 tablespoons lime juice

½ teaspoon dried chilli flakes

1 medium beetroot (beet) (160g), peeled, cut into 5mm (¼-inch) pieces

1 large carrot (180g), unpeeled, cut into 5mm (¼-inch) pieces

160g (5 ounces) snake beans, cut into 5mm (¼-inch) pieces

1 large lebanese cucumber (160g), halved lengthways

¼ cup (50g) jasmine rice

200g (6½ ounces) small cherry tomatoes, halved

3 green onions (scallions), sliced thinly

½ cup finely chopped fresh mint

2 tablespoons finely chopped fresh thai basil or coriander (cilantro)

⅓ cup (45g) roasted unsalted peanuts, chopped finely

1 medium butter (boston) lettuce, leaves separated

1 Preheat oven to 180°C/350°F.
2 Combine fish sauce, juice and chilli flakes in a large bowl.
3 Combine beetroot and 1 tablespoon of the dressing in a small bowl. Combine carrot, snake beans and 2 tablespoons of the dressing in a medium bowl. Remove seeds from cucumber; cut into 5mm (¼-inch) pieces. Add cucumber to remaining dressing in large bowl. Cover each bowl with plastic wrap; stand vegetables for 15 minutes.
4 Meanwhile, place rice on an oven tray; roast for 12 minutes or until golden. Process rice in a small food processor (or crush with a mortar and pestle) until very finely chopped.
5 Add tomatoes to cucumber mixture with onion, herbs, ground rice, carrot mixture and half the nuts. Strain beetroot mixture through a sieve, add to larb; toss gently to combine.
6 Serve larb with lettuce leaves, sprinkled with remaining nuts.

prep + cook time 30 minutes **serves** 4 as a side dish
nutritional count per serving 5.8g total fat (0.8g saturated fat); 781kJ (187 cal); 21.2g carbohydrate; 7.8g protein; 8.1g fibre

tip You will need about half a small bunch of snake beans for this recipe.

This zippy lasagne packs in the flavour with plenty of green vegetables, layered with a tangy, but healthy cheat's béchamel and wholemeal pasta.

pea, fennel and spinach lasagne

¼ cup (60ml) extra virgin olive oil

1 medium bulb fennel (300g), chopped finely

2 cloves garlic, crushed

2 shallots (50g), chopped finely

1 teaspoon ground fennel

2 teaspoons finely grated lemon rind

500g (1 pound) english spinach, trimmed

1½ cups (240g) fresh peas

1.2kg (2½ pounds) canned chopped tomatoes

1 cup roughly torn fresh basil leaves

250g (8 ounces) wholemeal lasagne sheets

¼ cup (60g) soft ricotta

2 tablespoons extra virgin olive oil, extra

¼ cup small basil leaves, extra

ricotta béchamel

1¾ cups (420g) soft ricotta

3 free-range eggs

½ cup (140g) Greek-style yoghurt

¼ cup (60ml) lemon juice

1 cup (200g) crumbled fetta

½ cup (125ml) sparkling mineral water

1 Heat 1½ tablespoons of the oil in a large frying pan over medium heat; cook fennel, garlic, shallots and ground fennel, stirring, for 8 minutes or until lightly golden. Transfer mixture to a large bowl; stir in rind. Season to taste.
2 Wash spinach leaves but don't dry. Cook spinach in same pan over high heat, in two batches, until wilted; drain. When cool enough to handle, squeeze out excess liquid. Coarsely chop spinach; stir into fennel mixture. Season to taste. Refrigerate until cooled. Stir in peas.
3 Preheat oven to 200°C/400°F.
4 Combine tomatoes, basil and remaining oil in a bowl; season.
5 Make ricotta béchamel.
6 Spread one-third of the tomato mixture over the base of a 3 litre (12-cup) baking dish. Cover with one-third of the pasta sheets. Top with half the spinach mixture and half the ricotta béchamel. Continue layering with remaining pasta sheets, tomato mixture, spinach mixture and ricotta béchamel, finishing with pasta sheets and tomato mixture. Top with spoonfuls of ricotta.
7 Bake lasagne for 45 minutes or until top is golden and pasta is cooked (cover with greased foil if necessary to prevent overbrowning). Stand for 10 minutes before serving. Serve lasagne drizzled with extra oil and topped with extra basil.
ricotta béchamel Whisk ricotta, eggs, yoghurt, juice and fetta in a large bowl until combined. Whisk mineral water into mixture until combined.

prep + cook time 1 hour 10 minutes (+ cooling) **serves** 6
nutritional count per serving 35g total fat (13.5g saturated fat); 2637kJ (630 cal); 43.6g carbohydrate; 29.3g protein; 11.8g fibre

Water spinach is a delicious asian green with small elongated leaves and succulent hollow stems. Both the mild-tasting stems and leaves are eaten.

stir-fried pumpkin, water spinach and tomatoes with five spice

¼ cup (60g) extra virgin coconut oil, melted

650g (1¼ pounds) jap pumpkin, peeled, cut into 3cm (1¼-inch) pieces

2 teaspoons chinese five-spice powder

¼ cup (60ml) oyster sauce

¼ cup (60ml) water

6cm (2½-inch) piece fresh ginger (30g), cut into fine matchsticks

185g (6 ounces) water spinach, trimmed, cut into thirds

250g (8 ounces) cherry tomatoes, halved

⅓ cup (20g) flaked almonds, roasted

1 Heat 2 tablespoons of the coconut oil in a large wok over medium heat; cook pumpkin pieces, turning frequently, for 6 minutes until almost tender. Remove from wok.
2 Meanwhile, combine five-spice, oyster sauce and the water in a small bowl.
3 Heat remaining oil in wok over medium-high heat; stir-fry ginger for 1 minute or until crisp. Add water spinach, tomatoes and five-spice mixture; stir-fry for 1 minute or until water spinach wilts. Return pumpkin to wok; stir through.
4 Serve stir-fry topped with almonds.

prep + cook time 15 minutes **serves** 4
nutritional count per serving 18.5g total fat (14g saturated fat); 1119kJ (267 cal); 17.6g carbohydrate; 4.6g protein; 6.5g fibre

tips Coconut oil is a solidified oil sold in jars and is available from major supermarkets and health food stores. Melt coconut oil as you would butter, either in a small saucepan over low heat or in the microwave. You will need about 1 bunch of water spinach for this recipe.

Fast-cooking clams are packed with a good dose of iron, B vitamins and the mineral chronium, which the body needs to regulate blood glucose levels. They need to be soaked in salted water first to purge them of any sand.

spelt spaghetti with cherry tomato sauce and vongole

You will need to soak the vongole (clams) in salted water for 30 minutes before you start this recipe.

1 bunch fresh basil (80g)

950g (2 pounds) heirloom cherry tomatoes, halved

1 medium lemon (140g), cut into 8 wedges

¼ cup (60ml) olive oil

375g (12 ounces) spelt spaghetti

1 medium red onion (170g), chopped finely

3 cloves garlic, sliced thinly

1kg (2 pounds) vongole (clams)

¾ cup (180ml) dry white wine

1 Preheat oven to 200°C/400°F.
2 Pick leaves from bunch of basil; reserve 1 cup of the smallest leaves (keep remaining leaves for another use). Tie basil stalks together with kitchen string. Place tomatoes, lemon wedges and basil stalks in a baking dish with 2 tablespoons of the oil; season, then toss to coat. Roast for 15 minutes or until tomatoes soften. Discard basil stalks. Squeeze juice from lemon wedges over tomatoes; discard wedges. Mash half the tomatoes with a fork.
3 Meanwhile, cook pasta in a large saucepan of boiling water or until almost tender.
4 Heat remaining oil in a large, deep frying pan over medium-high heat; cook onion and garlic, stirring, for 5 minutes or until softened. Add vongole and wine; boil, stirring, for 1 minute. Cook, covered, for 5 minutes or until vongole just open. Add tomato mixture, spaghetti and three-quarters of the reserved basil leaves, then season; toss to combine.
5 Serve in bowls topped with remaining basil leaves.

prep + cook time 30 minutes **serves** 4
nutritional count per serving 15.4g total fat (2.3g saturated fat); 2416kJ (577 cal); 77.5g carbohydrate; 24g protein; 9g fibre

tips You can use wholemeal spaghetti instead of the spelt spaghetti if you like. If you are a chilli fan, simply add 1 fresh long finely chopped red chilli with the onion in step 4.

Tomatoes contain the carotenoid lycopene, an antioxidant that gives them their red colour, and may be useful in reducing the risk of some cancers and heart disease. While cooking does slightly reduce the vitamin C content in tomatoes, it actually increases the lycopene content.

roasted tomato and white bean soup

1kg (2 pounds) ripe roma (egg) tomatoes, quartered

1 medium red onion (170g), cut into wedges

6 cloves garlic, unpeeled

1 tablespoon maple syrup

½ cup (125ml) extra virgin olive oil

⅓ cup loosely packed sage leaves

400g (12½ ounces) canned cannellini beans, drained, rinsed

2 cups (500ml) water

1 Preheat oven to 200°C/400°F.
2 Place tomatoes, onion and garlic in a roasting pan. Combine maple syrup and half the oil in a bowl, season to taste; pour over vegetables, then toss to coat. Roast for 45 minutes or until tomatoes are very soft and coloured at the edges.
3 Meanwhile, heat remaining oil in a small frying pan over medium heat; fry sage leaves, stirring for 1½ minutes or until crisp. Remove with a slotted spoon; drain on paper towel. Reserve sage oil.
4 Peel roasted garlic. Blend garlic, onion, two-thirds of the tomatoes and two-thirds of the beans until smooth. Pour mixture into a large saucepan with the water and remaining beans; cook over medium heat, stirring occasionally until warmed through. Season to taste.
5 Ladle soup into bowls. Top with remaining tomatoes and crisp sage leaves; drizzle with reserved sage oil.

prep + cook time 1 hour 10 minutes **serves** 4
nutritional count per serving 29g total fat (4.6g saturated fat); 1595kJ (381 cal); 18.9g carbohydrate; 7.6g protein; 8g fibre

A large number of quality scientific studies have provided strong evidence that consumption of brassica vegetables reduces the risk of cancer, particularly of the gastro-intestinal tract and lung.

Eating
brassicas regularly can help to protect you from other chronic diseases that affect us as we age, including Alzheimer's, cataracts and age-related macular degeneration, and certain aspects of functional decline. Yes, eating more broccoli just might help keep you looking and feeling younger for longer.

THERE
ARE BENEFITS TO CONSUMING BOTH RAW AND COOKED BRASSICAS. WHEN YOU COOK THEM YOU IMPROVE THE UPTAKE OF ANTIOXIDANTS INTO THE BLOODSTREAM FOR USE AROUND THE BODY. WHEN YOU CONSUME THE RAW VEG, MORE INTACT PLANT CELLS REACH THE COLON WHERE THE RESIDENT BACTERIA BREAK THE CELLS DOWN RELEASING THE ANTIOXIDANTS WHERE THEY CAN BENEFIT THE HEALTH OF COLONIC CELLS. RAW VEG MIGHT THEREFORE BE BETTER FOR REDUCING YOUR RISK OF BOWEL CANCER. WE THEREFORE RECOMMEND BOTH.

Throw raw broccoli florets into your salad, or finely slice raw Brussels sprouts and cabbage to make a crunchy 'slaw'.

brassicas

Brassicas are a family of vegetables that include broccoli, broccolini, cauliflower, brussels sprouts and cabbage (kale is also a brassica, but we've featured it on page 83). They deserve a superfood page all of their own because they are especially protective against cancer and heart disease.

Lightly
steaming or stir-frying are the best ways to preserve the nutrients present in your veg. You can also throw them into dishes in the last few moments of cooking until just softened. Brassicas are best eaten in this way. If you cook them too long they won't taste very nice and they'll lose their bright green colour.

How do
they do it? Brassicas are notably high in vitamins A, C and E, folate and potassium. All of these nutrients undoubtedly contribute towards the protective effect of these vegies. But it is the presence of particular phytochemicals that makes brassicas special. They contain a group of antioxidants called flavonoids, and a whole bunch of sulphur containing compounds including glucosinolates, which act as anti-cancer agents and ramp up detoxifying enzyme systems.

versatile vegies 115

Avocados are grown year round in Australia with varieties peaking at different times. One of the tastiest is hass, with creamy flesh, an oval shape and pebbly dark skin as it ripens. To check if avocados are ripe, squeeze the neck end gently.

chilled avocado soup with crab

3 fresh jalapeños or long green chillies

3 green onions (scallions), white and green parts

2 cloves garlic

125g (4 ounces) yellow grape tomatoes

2 tablespoons extra virgin olive oil

¼ cup fresh coriander (cilantro), torn

120g (4 ounces) cooked fresh crab meat

⅓ cup (80ml) lime juice

1 cup (250ml) water

2 medium avocados (500g), chopped

¾ cup (210g) Greek-style yoghurt

1 Preheat oven to 200°C/400°F.
2 Cut two of the chillies in half lengthways. Place in a roasting pan with the white part of onion, garlic, tomatoes and half the oil, season with salt; toss to coat. Roast for 15 minutes or until chillies are soft. Cool.
3 Meanwhile, remove seeds from remaining chilli; chop finely. Thinly slice the green part of the onion. Combine chopped chilli, sliced green onion, coriander, crab and remaining oil in a medium bowl. Cover; refrigerate until ready to serve.
4 Blend roasted vegetables with juice, the water, avocado and yoghurt until smooth. Season to taste. Refrigerate until chilled.
5 Ladle chilled soup into bowls; top with crab mixture. Season with freshly ground black pepper.

prep + cook time 20 minutes (+ refrigeration)
serves 6 as a starter
nutritional count per serving 20.8g total fat (5g saturated fat); 1027kJ (245 cal); 6.3g carbohydrate; 6.4g protein; 2.8g fibre

tips If you want to reduce the intensity of the chillies, remove their seeds and membranes before roasting. You can use chopped prawns or diced scallops instead of the crab meat if you like. You will need 3 limes for this recipe.

avocado pesto with prawns and pasta

375g (12 ounces) wholemeal penne

340g (11 ounces) asparagus, trimmed, halved crossways

2½ cups firmly packed fresh basil leaves

¼ cup (40g) pine nuts, toasted

1 clove garlic, crushed

2 tablespoons extra virgin olive oil

¼ cup (60ml) lemon juice

1 tablespoon water

1 medium avocado (250g), chopped

150g (4½ ounces) fetta

1kg (2 pounds) cooked tiger prawns (shrimp), shelled, deveined, with tails intact

⅓ cup lightly packed fresh small basil leaves, extra

1 Cook pasta in a large saucepan of boiling salted water for 8 minutes or until almost tender. Add asparagus; cook a further 1 minute until tender. Drain. Rinse under cold water; drain.
2 Meanwhile, process basil, pine nuts, garlic, oil, juice and the water until finely chopped. Add avocado and half the fetta; process until smooth. Season to taste.
3 Place pasta, asparagus and pesto mixture in a large bowl with prawns; toss gently to combine.
4 Divide pasta among bowls; top with remaining fetta and extra basil leaves.

prep + cook time 25 minutes   **serves** 4
nutritional count per serving 37.2g total fat (10.2g saturated fat); 3311kJ (791 cal); 59.5g carbohydrate; 48g protein; 12.7g fibre

tip Asparagus spears vary in thickness; if the ends are really thick, peel them from the bottom up to within 5cm (2 inches) of the tips.

kumara, eggplant and coconut curry

650g (1¼ pounds) finger eggplants

olive oil spray

2 tablespoons olive oil

1 large onion (200g), chopped finely

4cm (1½-inch) piece fresh ginger (20g), chopped finely

1 fresh small red chilli, chopped finely

2 cloves garlic, crushed

4 cardamom pods, crushed lightly

1 teaspoon garam marsala

1 teaspoon ground cumin

1 teaspoon ground turmeric

800g (1½ pounds) kumara (orange sweet potato), cut into 3cm (1¼-inch) pieces

270ml (9 fluid ounces) canned coconut milk

400g (12½ ounces) canned diced tomatoes

1 cup (250ml) vegetable stock

2 tablespoons olive oil, extra

1 tablespoon brown mustard seeds

24 fresh curry leaves

400g (12½ ounces) tuscan cabbage (cavalo nero), chopped coarsely

2 tablespoons water

1 Preheat oven to 180°C/350°F. Line two oven trays with baking paper.
2 Quarter eggplants lengthways; place on trays, spray with oil. Bake for 20 minutes or until golden and soft.
3 Heat olive oil in a large saucepan over medium-high heat; cook onion, ginger, chilli and garlic for 3 minutes. Reduce heat to low, add cardamom, garam marsala, cumin and turmeric; cook for 2 minutes. Increase heat to medium, add kumara; stir to coat in spices.
4 Add coconut milk to pan with tomatoes and stock; bring to the boil. Reduce heat; simmer, covered, for 20 minutes or until kumara is tender. Stir in eggplant; return to the boil. Season to taste.
5 Meanwhile, heat extra oil in a large frying pan over medium-high heat; cook mustard seeds, stirring, for 1 minute or until seeds pop. Add curry leaves; cook 1 minute. Stir in cabbage and the water; cook, covered until just wilted. Season to taste.
6 Serve curry with cabbage mixture.

prep + cook time 1 hour **serves** 6
nutritional count per serving 23.6g total fat (10.2g saturated fat); 1642kJ (392 cal); 32.7g carbohydrate; 7.9g protein; 10g fibre

serving suggestion Serve with steamed basmati rice and yoghurt.

Garlic stands out as having particularly potent anti-cancer effects. It has high levels of allicin and other sulphur compounds that are thought to be responsible. Garlic is also anti-bacterial, it can block the formation of carcinogenic substances, can enhance the repair of DNA in cells around the body and can assist in killing off rogue cells that may progress to cancer. The World Health Organization recommends we eat a clove of garlic a day for general health.

Does cooking affect the benefits?

High heat, prolonged storage and exposure to light are known to affect the levels and form of the potentially beneficial substances in garlic. But on the other hand, raw garlic disagrees with many people. You might find that raw garlic repeats on you and garlic breath is not so desirable. Or you may find it causes heartburn or indigestion. Since there are many studies showing a benefit of cooked and raw garlic, as well as other cooked allium vegetables, there is clearly still a benefit from enjoying them in this way. What you might like to do is rather than frying your garlic at the start of the dish, try adding it a little later to the pan to reduce the heat exposure.

alliums

The alliums are the onion family of vegetables that includes onions, leeks, garlic, green onions (or shallots), spring onions and eschalots. These vegetables have been associated with a lower risk of several cancers, including cancer of the stomach, colon, oesophagus, pancreas, breast, prostate and brain.

You have no doubt heard of probiotics – healthy bacteria that we need to colonise the gut – well, research suggests that prebiotics might be more important. These are compounds in food that act as specific fuel to these good bacteria. Having prebiotics in your diet therefore encourages the growth of healthy bacterial populations and pushes out the bad guys. Alliums provide a particular group of these prebiotics called fructo-oligosaccharides (FOS).

FRUCTO-OLIGOSACCHARIDES (FOS) CAN CAUSE PROBLEMS FOR PEOPLE WITH IRRITABLE BOWEL DISEASE (IBS), BUT THAT MAY BE DUE TO HAVING AN IMBALANCE OF BACTERIAL GROUPS PRESENT, WITH MORE OF THE BAD GUYS. SEE A DIETITIAN OR OTHER HEALTH PROFESSIONAL FOR MORE ADVICE.

THE BOTTOM LINE is, however you enjoy alliums, get them into your daily menu. Use them in cooking, throw them raw into salads or crush a clove of garlic into a salad dressing.

Numerous studies have shown that members of the brassica family, which includes cauliflower and tuscan cabbage offer some protection against cancers, heart disease and the functional declines associated with ageing.

cauliflower and tomato gratin

¼ cup (60ml) olive oil

1kg (2 pounds) cauliflower, cut into small florets

2 medium onions (300g), chopped finely

3 cloves garlic, crushed

½ teaspoon saffron threads

800g (1½ pounds) canned diced tomatoes

¼ cup (40g) currants

200g (7 ounces) tuscan cabbage (cavalo nero), shredded

¼ cup coarsely chopped fresh flat-leaf parsley

topping

250g (8 ounces) spelt or wholegrain bread, torn coarsely

¼ cup (35g) pine nuts

¼ cup (35g) sunflower seeds

¼ cup (50g) pepitas (pumpkin seeds)

2 tablespoons sesame seeds

½ cup (40g) grated pecorino cheese

1 clove garlic, chopped

¼ cup (60ml) olive oil

1 Heat 2 tablespoons of the oil in a large deep, frying pan over medium heat; cook cauliflower, covered, stirring occasionally, for 6 minutes or until starting to colour. Remove from pan.
2 Heat remaining oil in same pan; cook onion and garlic, covered, for 3 minutes. Add saffron, tomatoes and currants; bring to a simmer. Return cauliflower to pan with cabbage and parsley; cook, stirring, until cabbage just wilts. Season to taste.
3 Preheat oven to 180°C/350°F.
4 Make topping.
5 Spoon cauliflower mixture into a 3 litre (12-cup) ovenproof dish; cover evenly with topping mixture. Bake for 35 minutes or until topping is crisp and golden.
topping Combine ingredients in a medium bowl.

prep + cook time 1 hour **serves** 6
nutritional count per serving 35.7g total fat (5.8g saturated fat); 2249kJ (537 cal); 31.5g carbohydrate; 16.5g protein; 13.3g fibre

tip Pecorino is a hard Italian sheep's milk cheese similar to parmesan which may be used instead if you like.

spicy roast pumpkin with lamb

¾ cup (150g) cracked wheat
2 tablespoons coarsely chopped fresh flat-leaf parsley
2 tablespoons coarsely chopped fresh thyme
2 tablespoons finely grated lemon rind
2 cloves garlic, crushed
2 tablespoons olive oil
1.4kg (2¾-pound) small jap pumpkin, unpeeled, cut into small wedges
1 cup (280g) Greek-style yoghurt
2 teaspoons sumac
6 thyme sprigs, torn, extra

lamb topping
1 tablespoon olive oil
1 medium onion (150g), chopped finely
1 teaspoon ground cinnamon
½ teaspoon cayenne pepper
300g (9½ ounces) minced (ground) lamb
1 tablespoon pomegranate molasses

1 Cook cracked wheat in a medium saucepan of boiling water for 10 minutes (it will not be quite cooked). Drain; rinse. Place wheat in a medium bowl; cool for 15 minutes. Stir in chopped herbs, rind, garlic and oil; season to taste.
2 Preheat oven to 180°C/350°F. Line a large oven tray with baking paper.
3 Place pumpkin wedges, skin-side down, on oven tray; spoon wheat mixture into the hollow of each wedge. Bake, uncovered, for 30 minutes; cover with foil, bake a further 30 minutes or until pumpkin is tender.
4 Meanwhile, make lamb topping.
5 Spoon lamb topping over pumpkin wedges; serve topped with yoghurt, sumac and extra thyme.
lamb topping Heat oil in a frying pan over medium heat; cook onion, cinnamon and cayenne, stirring for 3 minutes. Increase heat to high, add lamb; cook, stirring occasionally, for 5 minutes or until browned and cooked through. Stir in molasses; season to taste.

prep + cook time 1 hour 30 minutes **serves** 6
nutritional count per serving 19.8g total fat (6g saturated fat); 1851kJ (442 cal); 42g carbohydrate; 18.9g protein; 10.3g fibre

seeded carrot and cabbage fillo pie

¼ cup (60ml) olive oil

1 small leek (200g), white part only, sliced thinly

2 cloves garlic, crushed

2 teaspoons caraway seeds

2 medium carrots (270g), grated coarsely

250g (8 ounces) savoy cabbage, shredded

¼ cup (40g) currants

2 tablespoons finely chopped fresh mint

14 sheets fillo pastry (210g)

⅓ cup (80ml) olive oil, extra

topping

¼ cup (50g) pepitas (pumpkin seeds)

¼ cup (35g) slivered almonds

¼ cup (25g) coarsely chopped walnuts

1 tablespoon poppy seeds

1 tablespoon sesame seeds

herb salad

2 small lebanese cucumbers (260g)

1 cup fresh flat-leaf parsley leaves

1 cup fresh curly parsley leaves

½ cup fresh mint leaves

½ cup fresh dill sprigs

2 green onions (scallions), sliced thinly

1 tablespoon red wine vinegar

2 tablespoons olive oil

75g (2½ ounces) soft goat's cheese, crumbled

1 Heat oil in a large frying pan over medium heat; cook leek, garlic and seeds for 5 minutes. Add carrot; cook for 3 minutes. Add cabbage; cook a further 5 minutes or until vegetables are soft. Stir in currants and mint. Cool.
2 Make topping.
3 Preheat oven to 180°C/350°F.
4 Divide filling into seven portions. Brush one sheet of pastry with a little of the extra oil; top with a second sheet. Keep remaining sheets covered with a clean, damp tea towel. Place one portion of filling lengthways, in a thin line, along pastry edge; roll pastry over filling. Starting at the centre of a 24cm (9½-inch) springform pan, carefully form the pastry roll, seam-side down, into a coil. Repeat with remaining pastry, oil and filling, joining each roll to the end of the last one and coiling it around until the base of the pan is covered. Brush top with oil.
5 Bake fillo pie for 18 minutes. Evenly cover with topping; bake a further 8 minutes or until golden.
6 Meanwhile, make herb salad.
7 Serve fillo pie with herb salad.
topping Combine ingredients in a small bowl.
herb salad Using a vegetable peeler, peel cucumbers into ribbons. Place cucumber in a medium bowl with herbs, onion, vinegar and oil; toss gently to combine. Top with cheese.

prep + cook time 1 hour **serves** 6
nutritional count per serving 30.9g total fat (5.5g saturated fat); 2032kJ (485 cal); 33.8g carbohydrate; 13.5g protein; 10.4g fibre

After eating chilli, pain-relieving endorphins are released into the brain. This may explain why some people get a little bit addicted to the heat from chillies.

HALF A CAPSICUM PROVIDES A GOOD DOSE OF FOLATE, ABOUT 7% OF YOUR DAILY NEED, AND ROUGHLY 8% OF YOUR VITAMIN B6. BOTH OF THESE VITAMINS ARE INVOLVED IN REDUCING BLOOD LEVELS OF THE AMINO ACID HOMOCYSTEINE. RAISED HOMOCYSTEINE HAS BEEN ASSOCIATED WITH AN INCREASED RISK OF CARDIOVASCULAR DISEASE. VITAMIN B6 IS ALSO NECESSARY FOR PROTEIN METABOLISM, FOR HEALTHY RADIANT SKIN AND GOOD IMMUNE FUNCTION.

capsicum & chilli

The chemical responsible for heat of a spicy chilli is capsaicin. This fiery little compound has many potential benefits in the body. It increases the body's production of heat and can help to clear nasal congestion, making it a great winter food. Capsaicin may also be able to kill off rogue cancer cells and help to detoxify cancer-causing agents.

It's not only oranges that are fabulous for vitamin C, half a red capsicum gives you well over your entire daily requirement. Vitamin C is one of the major antioxidants and an essential player in supporting optimal immune function.

Capsicum also provide an array of carotenoids, including beta-carotene, with antioxidant functions. Some can also be converted to vitamin A in the body, a nutrient that is critical for good vision and healthy eyes. Since it is also necessary for new cell formation, vitamin A is essential for healthy skin and many organs including the heart, lungs, liver and kidneys.

Toasting nuts and seeds amplifies their flavour and will freshen them up if they're a little on the stale side. Toast the sesame seeds in a heavy-based frying pan without any oil over medium heat, stirring continuously, for 3 minutes or until they're evenly golden.

broccoli and ocean trout salad

600g (1¼ pounds) broccoli florets

2 tablespoons olive oil

350g (12 ounces) brussels sprouts, halved

3 green onions (scallions), sliced thinly

½ cup (75g) dry-roasted cashews, chopped coarsely

1 tablespoon sesame seeds, toasted

1 medium nashi pear (200g), cored, sliced thinly

200g (7-ounce) skinless, boneless ocean trout fillet

2 tablespoons rice flour or cornflour (cornstarch)

2 tablespoons peanut oil

dressing

1 tablespoon sesame oil

1 tablespoon olive oil

¼ cup (60ml) rice wine vinegar

1 clove garlic, crushed

¼ teaspoon cayenne pepper

1 tablespoon soy sauce

1 Make dressing.
2 Cook broccoli in a large saucepan of boiling water 1 minute; drain. Refresh under cold water; drain. Pat broccoli dry with paper towel.
3 Heat half the olive oil in a large frying pan over medium-high heat; cook sprouts, cut-side down, for 2 minutes or until golden. Turn over; cook a further minute or until almost tender. Remove from pan.
4 Heat remaining oil in same frying pan; cook broccoli for 3 minutes or until browned lightly and warmed.
5 Place sprouts and broccoli in a large bowl with onion, nuts, sesame seeds, pear and dressing; toss gently to combine.
6 Cut trout into 1cm (½-inch) slices. Dust slices in rice flour; shake off excess. Heat peanut oil in same frying pan over high heat; cook trout for 1 minute each side or until golden and cooked through. Drain on paper towel.
7 Serve salad topped with flaked pieces of trout.
dressing Place ingredients in a screw-top jar; shake well.

prep + cook time 35 minutes **serves** 6
nutritional count per serving 30.1g total fat (5g saturated fat); 1601kJ (382 cal); 9.9g carbohydrate; 14.1g protein; 6.6g fibre

Beetroot stems are tender and sweet like silver beet and the slightly sour leaves are also edible. Little is wasted in this clever tart that utilises all parts of the beetroot.

roast beetroot, garlic and chia seed tart

500g (1 pound) baby beetroot (beets), stems and leaves attached

8 cloves garlic, unpeeled

6 sprigs fresh thyme

2½ tablespoons olive oil

3 medium red onions (510g), sliced thinly

60g (2 ounces) soft goat's cheese, crumbled

1 clove garlic, crushed, extra

2 tablespoons extra virgin olive oil

2 tablespoons orange juice

1 teaspoon white chia seeds

pastry

2 tablespoons white chia seeds

2 tablespoons warm water

1½ cups (240g) wholemeal plain (all-purpose) flour

1 teaspoon sea salt flakes

50g (1½ ounces) cold unsalted butter, chopped

1 free-range egg

¼ cup (60ml) olive oil

1 Trim beetroot, leaving a little of the stems attached. Finely chop enough of the beetroot stems to make up 2 tablespoons; reserve for the pastry. Pick 20g (¾ ounce) small beetroot leaves, cover with damp paper towel; refrigerate until ready to use. Pick a further 100g (3 ounces) of beetroot leaves, shred finely; refrigerate. Discard remaining leaves and stems.
2 Make pastry.
3 Preheat oven to 200°C/400°F. Line an oven tray with foil.
4 Place beetroot, garlic and thyme in the centre of the tray; drizzle with 2 teaspoons of the oil. Wrap foil around beetroot. Roast 20 minutes; check garlic, remove if tender when lightly squeezed. Roast beetroot a further 10 minutes or until tender; discard thyme. Peel beetroot; cut into quarters.
5 Meanwhile, heat remaining oil in a large frying pan over low heat; cook onions, stirring occasionally, for 20 minutes or until very soft. Add shredded leaves; stir for 3 minutes or until wilted. Season to taste. Cool.
6 Roll pastry between sheets of baking paper into a 30cm (12-inch) round. Using a bowl as a guide, trim pastry into a 29cm (11¾-inch) round. Fold in the edge to create a 1cm (½-inch) border.
7 Slide pastry with the paper onto a large oven tray; bake for 12 minutes or until golden. Spread onion mixture on tart base; top with roasted beetroot and garlic and cheese. Bake a further 10 minutes or until cheese is golden.
8 Whisk extra garlic, extra virgin olive oil and juice in a small bowl; season to taste. Add reserved small beetroot leaves; toss to coat. Top tart with beetroot leaves; sprinkle with chia seeds.
pastry Combine chia seeds and the water in a medium bowl; stand for 20 minutes. Add flour, salt and butter; rub together until mixture resembles coarse crumbs. Stir in reserved beetroot stems (from step 1). Whisk egg and oil in a small bowl, add to flour mixture; mix with your hands until just combined. Shape pastry into a disc. Cover; refrigerate 30 minutes.

prep + cook time 1 hour 15 minutes (+ standing & refrigeration)
serves 4
nutritional count per serving 54g total fat (15.2g saturated fat); 3359kJ (802 cal); 54.1g carbohydrate; 17.8g protein; 17.4g fibre

tip You could also use 2 bunches of small beetroot. You will need to roast them for 1¼ hours and cut them into wedges.

super seafood

An abundance of scientific research shows the benefits of eating more fish and seafood in our diet.

You can use four 250g (8-ounce) pieces of salmon fillet instead of the barramundi, if you like. You will need to reduce the cooking time slightly.

baked baby barramundi with pumpkin seed pesto

480g (15½ ounces) asparagus

300g (9½ ounces) green beans

4 x 340g (11-ounce) plate-size farmed barramundi

2 medium lemons (280g), sliced thinly

¼ cup (60ml) olive oil

pumpkin seed pesto

1 cup (200g) pepitas (pumpkin seeds)

2 cups firmly packed fresh basil leaves

1 clove garlic, crushed

1 tablespoon finely grated lemon rind

¼ cup (60ml) lemon juice

⅓ cup (80ml) olive oil

¼ cup (60ml) water

1 Preheat oven to 220°C/425°F. Line two large oven trays with baking paper.
2 Divide asparagus and beans between trays. Cut three slashes crossways into the thickest part of each fish on both sides; place on vegetables. Top fish with lemon slices, drizzle with olive oil; season.
3 Bake fish and vegetables for 25 minutes or until fish is cooked through (the flesh in the slits will appear opaque).
4 Meanwhile, make pumpkin seed pesto.
5 Divide fish and vegetables among plates; serve with pesto.
pumpkin seed pesto Process pepitas, basil, garlic, rind and juice until well combined. With the motor operating, gradually add combined oil and the water; process until smooth.

prep + cook time 40 minutes **serves** 4
nutritional count per serving 57.1g total fat (9.3g saturated fat); 3301kJ (788 cal); 11g carbohydrate; 54.2g protein; 9.5g fibre

tip If you have both trays in the oven at the same time, to ensure even cooking, either swap the trays halfway through cooking time or use the oven's fan-forced function (you will need to reduce the temperature to 200°C/400°F).

Sashimi-grade fish must be impeccably fresh and prepared using extremely strict standards of hygiene as the fish is to be eaten raw. If you are unable to obtain it, or prefer your fish cooked, simply cook the fish for a further 1½ minutes on each side or until cooked through.

seared wasabi salmon and brown rice salad

500g (1 pound) packaged pre-cooked brown basmati rice

350g (11 ounces) sashimi-grade salmon

2 tablespoons sesame seeds

1 tablespoon wasabi powder

2 tablespoons olive oil

100g (3 ounces) baby asian salad leaves

¼ cup (70g) pickled ginger

2 green onions (scallions), sliced thinly

1 fresh long red chilli, sliced thinly

1 large avocado (320g), chopped

2 tablespoons light soy sauce

2 tablespoons lime juice

1 tablespoon olive oil, extra

1 lime, cut into wedges

1 Reheat rice following packet instructions; cool slightly.
2 Meanwhile, roll salmon in combined sesame seeds and wasabi powder until coated.
3 Heat oil in a large frying pan over high heat; cook salmon for 1 minute each side or until browned but still raw in the centre. Cool for 5 minutes. Cut into thin slices.
4 Place brown rice in a large bowl with salad leaves, ginger, onion, chilli and avocado; toss gently to combine.
5 Place sauce, juice and extra oil in a screw-top jar; shake well.
6 Arrange rice salad and salmon on a platter; drizzle with dressing. Serve with lime wedges.

prep + cook time 20 minutes **serves** 4
nutritional count per serving 41.6g total fat (8.4g saturated fat); 2893kJ (691 cal); 44.3g carbohydrate; 32g protein; 5.4g fibre

tips If you can't find wasabi powder, use the equivalent amount of wasabi paste and spread it over the salmon before rolling it in sesame seeds.

SALMON IS ALSO RICH IN PROTEIN AND A NEW AREA OF RESEARCH IS LOOKING AT THE POTENTIAL BENEFITS OF SOME OF THE PEPTIDES (SMALL PROTEINS) PRESENT. ONE IN PARTICULAR CALLED CALCITONIN IS GARNERING A LOT OF ATTENTION. WE MAKE OUR OWN FORM OF CALCITONIN IN THE THYROID GLAND, AND WE KNOW IT'S INVOLVED IN COLLAGEN FORMATION AND BONE METABOLISM. THIS NEW RESEARCH IS INVESTIGATING WHETHER THE CALCITONIN AND OTHER BIOACTIVE PEPTIDES IN SALMON MAY HAVE BENEFITS IN MAINTAINING HEALTHY JOINTS, BONE AND SLOWING THE AGEING OF THE SKIN. SALMON JUST MIGHT HELP TO KEEP US LOOKING YOUNGER.

The long chain omega-3 fats are anti-inflammatory and so can be useful in treating arthritis and may help to control asthma by lowering inflammation in the lungs. Salmon may have additional anti-inflammatory factors that make it a particularly 'super' food. It is one of the best sources of selenium and high intakes of this mineral have been associated with decreased risk of joint inflammation, as well as a lower risk of several types of cancer.

Omega-3s are good for your heart. They lower blood triglyceride levels and blood pressure.

atlantic salmon

Atlantic salmon ranks amongst the richest food sources of the long chain omega-3 fats EPA and DHA. Salmon is especially rich in DHA, the most abundant omega-3 fat in the brain and in the retina of the eye. DHA is therefore considered to be particularly important for brain function and general brain health.

Cultures that eat a lot of fish and seafood have lower levels of depression. There is ongoing research into this area, but there is certainly some evidence to suggest that upping the intake of omega-3s can help reduce depressive symptoms in some people.

Although we can make EPA and DHA from shorter chain omega-3 fats found in some plants, our capacity to do this is limited. To ensure we get optimal amounts we really need to consume sufficient amounts in our diet. To meet requirements, our health recommendations are to consume oily fish such as salmon at least a couple of times a week.

Harissa is a spicy North African condiment of chilli and spices. Recent research has shown countries with a high chilli consumption, such as Mexico and India tend to have decreased rates of cancer. Chillies also boost our metabolism, helping to burn fat and increase satiety.

harissa and tomato prawns with fetta

1 tablespoon olive oil

1 medium onion (150g), sliced thinly

2 cloves garlic, sliced thinly

¼ cup (60ml) dry white wine

20 uncooked banana prawns (shrimp) (700g), shelled, deveined, with tails intact

2 teaspoons harissa

400g (12½ ounces) canned diced tomatoes

2 tablespoons currants

1 teaspoon caster (superfine) sugar

2 cups (400g) whole wheat couscous

2 cups (500ml) boiling water

100g (3 ounces) greek fetta, crumbled

2 teaspoons olive oil, extra

2 tablespoons fresh flat-leaf parsley leaves

1 Preheat a grill (broiler) to high.
2 Heat oil in a large, deep ovenproof frying pan over medium heat; cook onion and garlic for 5 minutes or until tender. Add wine; cook over high heat for 30 seconds. Add prawns and harissa; cook, stirring occasionally, for 2 minutes. Add tomatoes, currants and sugar. Reduce heat to low; cook for 3 minutes or until prawns are just cooked. Season.
3 Meanwhile, place couscous and the boiling water in a large bowl. Cover with plastic wrap; stand for 5 minutes or until water is absorbed. Fluff couscous with a fork.
4 Scatter fetta on prawns; drizzle with extra oil. Place pan under grill for 2 minutes or until fetta is golden. Sprinkle with parsley. Serve prawns with couscous.

prep + cook time 25 minutes **serves** 4
nutritional count per serving 14.5g total fat (5g saturated fat); 2665kJ (637 cal); 89g carbohydrate; 34.8g protein; 2.8g fibre

tips If you don't like things too spicy, replace 1 teaspoon of harissa with 1 teaspoon cumin seeds. If you don't have an ovenproof frying pan, wrap the handle of your pan in several layers of foil.

Chervil is a delicately flavoured herb with anise overtones and a soft feathery texture. You can use coarsely chopped flat-leaf parsley instead.

oysters with cucumber and shallot salad

1 lebanese cucumber (130g), halved lengthways
1 shallot (25g), chopped finely
2 tablespoons champagne vinegar
1 teaspoon caster (superfine) sugar
2 tablespoons fresh chervil leaves
24 oysters on the half shell (720g)

1 Scrape out the seeds from the cucumber using a teaspoon; finely chop the cucumber.
2 Combine cucumber, shallot, vinegar, sugar and half the chervil in a small bowl.
3 Spoon salad onto oysters; top with remaining chervil.

prep time 10 minutes **serves** 4 as a starter
nutritional count per serving 1.4g total fat (0.4g saturated fat); 234kJ (56 cal); 2.2g carbohydrate; 7.5g protein; 0.7g fibre

tip You can use white balsamic vinegar instead of the champagne vinegar.

You can take a recipe short-cut by chopping the mint and parsley in the food processor, just make sure you use the pulse button. For those with a gluten intolerance, replace the wheat with 1 cup cooked quinoa, brown rice or millet.

baked salmon fillets with tahini sauce and tabbouleh

4 x 150g (4½-ounce) salmon fillets, skinned

1½ teaspoons sumac

2 tablespoons extra virgin olive oil

tabbouleh

½ cup (80g) coarse cracked wheat

1½ cups (375ml) water

2 green onions (scallions), sliced thinly

1 medium tomato (150g), chopped coarsely

1 cup firmly packed fresh flat-leaf parsley leaves, chopped coarsely

¼ cup firmly packed fresh mint leaves, chopped coarsely

1 tablespoon lemon juice

tahini sauce

½ cup (140g) Greek-style yoghurt

1½ tablespoons tahini

1 clove garlic, crushed

2 teaspoons lemon juice

1 Make tabbouleh, then tahini sauce.
2 Preheat oven to 200°C/400°F.
3 Line an oven tray with baking paper. Place salmon on tray, sprinkle with 1 teaspoon of the sumac; drizzle with oil. Season. Bake for 12 minutes or until almost cooked through.
4 Serve salmon with tahini sauce and tabbouleh. Sprinkle with remaining sumac.
tabbouleh Bring cracked wheat and the water to the boil in a small saucepan. Reduce heat to low; cook for 20 minutes or until tender. Drain. Place cracked wheat in a large bowl with onion, tomato, herbs and juice; toss to combine. Season.
tahini sauce Whisk ingredients in a small bowl until combined; season to taste.

prep + cook time 40 minutes **serves** 4
nutritional count per serving 35.3g total fat (8.4g saturated fat); 2520kJ (602 cal); 18.9g carbohydrate; 49.3g protein; 6g fibre

tip You can make the tabbouleh and tahini sauce several hours ahead; store in the refrigerator until ready to use.

Shellfish are rich in selenium – a mineral we need only tiny amounts of, but is often lacking in our diets due to low selenium levels in the soil. Selenium is necessary for thyroid hormone metabolism, to make DNA and to protect cells around the body from oxidative damage and infection.

If you don't like oysters, mussels and clams are not too far behind on the zinc front and are also iron rich – clams in particular are fantastic for iron. For those who choose not to eat red meat, tuck into shellfish on a regular basis to ensure you meet your body's requirement for both zinc and iron.

mussels, oysters & clams

The richest food source of zinc is oysters. Just one oyster provides approximately 10mg. The recommended intake for women is 8mg and men 14mg. It's not often our requirement for a mineral can be so easily met with a mouthful or two of one food.

A DOZEN MUSSELS PROVIDE ALL THE IRON AND VITAMIN B12 YOU NEED FOR THE DAY, A THIRD OF YOUR ZINC, MORE THAN A THIRD OF YOUR MAGNESIUM AND A TENTH OF YOUR VITAMIN A. AND ALL FOR ONLY 540 KILOJOULES AND PRETTY MUCH NO SATURATED FAT. MOST OF THOSE KILOJOULES COME FROM PROTEIN, SO OPTING FOR MUSSELS ON THE MENU CAN HELP WITH CURBING YOUR APPETITE AND CONTROLLING YOUR WEIGHT.

Sustainable choices

From a seafood sustainability point of view, mussels, oysters and other shellfish are considered some of the best choices. They have a green rating in the Australia's Sustainable Seafood Guide.

Only 'true' tarragon, the French variety, has a lovely anise-like flavour that pairs well with seafood. Although rarely labelled, French tarragon has distinguishing narrow leaves, while Russian tarragon has serrated leaves and yellow flowers. If unavailable increase the dill to ½ cup.

prawn, pea and broad bean frittata with lemon herb salad

½ cup fresh flat-leaf parsley leaves

⅓ cup fresh dill sprigs

¼ cup fresh tarragon leaves

6 free-range eggs

½ cup (125ml) buttermilk

2 tablespoons dried breadcrumbs

500g (1 pound) cooked medium prawns (shrimp)

2 tablespoons olive oil

2 medium zucchini (240g), halved lengthways, sliced thinly

3 green onions (scallions), sliced thinly

2 cloves garlic, crushed

2 cups (240g) frozen peas, thawed

2¼ cups (370g) frozen broad (fava) beans, peeled, thawed

⅓ cup (80g) ricotta

1 medium lemon (140g), segmented (see tip)

1 tablespoon baby salted capers, rinsed

1 Coarsely chop half the herbs. Reserve remaining herbs. Whisk chopped herbs, eggs, buttermilk and breadcrumbs in a large bowl; season.
2 Shell and devein prawns, leaving 6 prawns with tails intact.
3 Preheat oven to 180°C/350°F.
4 Heat oil in a 21cm (8½-inch) ovenproof frying pan over medium heat; cook zucchini and onion, stirring, for 5 minutes or until soft. Add garlic, peas and beans; cook, stirring, for 1 minute or until fragrant. Add egg mixture; gently shake pan to distribute mixture. Cook over medium-low heat, without stirring, for 5 minutes or until the edge is set. Add prawns, placing prawns with tails upright in pan. Top with ricotta. Bake frittata for 20 minutes or until the centre is just firm.
5 Meanwhile, combine reserved herbs, lemon segments and capers in a small bowl.
6 Serve frittata topped with lemon herb salad.

prep + cook time 1 hour **serves** 4
nutritional count per serving 20.6g total fat (5.6g saturated fat); 1733kJ (414 cal); 15.8g carbohydrate; 35.8g protein; 10.4g fibre

tips If you don't have an ovenproof frying pan, wrap the handle of you pan in several layers of foil. To segment a lemon, use a small sharp knife to cut the top and bottom from lemon. Cut off the rind with the white pith, following the curve of the fruit. Holding the lemon over a bowl, cut down both sides of the white membrane to release each segment.

A fish burger makes a delicious alternative to a beef burger and is a particularly good way to disguise fish for finicky eaters. You can use white-fleshed fish, or even prawns, instead of the salmon for something different.

salmon and zucchini burgers with green hummus

1 medium zucchini (120g), grated coarsely

¼ teaspoon salt

500g (1-pound) skinless, boneless salmon fillet, chopped coarsely

6 green onions (scallions), chopped finely

2 cloves garlic, crushed

1 free-range egg

1 teaspoon ground cumin

⅓ cup coarsely chopped fresh mint

⅓ cup coarsely chopped fresh flat-leaf parsley

⅓ cup coarsely chopped fresh dill

⅔ cup (50g) coarse fresh wholemeal breadcrumbs

½ cup (135g) hummus

2 tablespoon Greek-style yoghurt

2 tablespoons olive oil

½ baby cos (romaine) lettuce (80g)

2 medium tomatoes (300g), sliced thinly

4 wholegrain bread rolls (240g), split, toasted

1 Combine zucchini and salt in a small bowl; stand 5 minutes. Squeeze excess liquid from zucchini.
2 Pulse salmon in a food processor into 1cm (½-inch) pieces. Add zucchini, onion, garlic, egg, cumin and half the herbs; pulse until well combined (pulse in short quick bursts to ensure you don't overmix and make the mixture tough). Add breadcrumbs, pulse until combined; season. (The mixture will be quite wet but will firm on chilling.) Using damp hands, shape mixture into four 10cm (4-inch) patties. Place on a baking-paper-lined tray. Cover; refrigerate 30 minutes.
3 Meanwhile, to make green hummus, process hummus and remaining herbs in processor until smooth. Add yoghurt; pulse until combined.
4 Heat oil in a large frying pan over medium heat; cook patties for 3 minutes each side or until just cooked through.
5 Place lettuce, patties, green hummus and tomato between toasted rolls.

prep + cook time 40 minutes (+ refrigeration) **serves** 4
nutritional count per serving 33.8g total fat (7.4g saturated fat); 2482kJ (593 cal); 22.4g carbohydrate; 46g protein; 7.6g fibre

tip To make ⅔ cup fresh breadcrumbs, remove the crust from three 1.5cm (¾-inch) thick slices of wholemeal bread; process slices until they become coarse crumbs.

Cooking the fish next to the bay leaves will infuse it with a camphor-like flavour. You could also use citrus-scented kaffir lime leaves for an Asian flavour and continue the theme to the coleslaw by swapping pecans with peanuts, lemon juice with lime juice and parsley with coriander.

snapper and bay leaf skewers with root vegetable slaw

You will need to soak 8 bamboo skewers in water for about an hour before you start this recipe.

½ medium celeriac (celery root) (300g), peeled

1 medium red apple (150g), unpeeled

1 medium carrot (120g), unpeeled

250g (8 ounces) savoy cabbage, shredded finely

⅔ cup finely chopped fresh chives

¼ cup chopped fresh flat-leaf parsley

⅓ cup (40g) pecans, roasted, chopped coarsely

⅓ cup (80ml) buttermilk

⅓ cup (80ml) extra virgin olive oil

2 teaspoons lemon juice

1kg (2 pounds) thick snapper fillets, skinned, trimmed

24 large fresh bay leaves

1 tablespoon olive oil

1 medium lemon (140g), cut into wedges

1 To make slaw, using a mandoline or V-slicer, slice celeriac, apple and carrot into matchsticks. Place sliced vegetables in a large bowl with cabbage, herbs and nuts. Add combined buttermilk, extra virgin olive oil and juice, then season; toss gently to combine.

2 Cut snapper into 16 even pieces (about 5cm/2 inches each) avoiding any bones. Thread 3 bay leaves and 2 pieces of snapper alternately onto each skewer. Brush snapper with olive oil; season.

3 Cook skewers on a heated grill plate (or grill or barbecue) over medium heat for 2 minutes each side or until just cooked through.

4 Serve skewers with slaw and lemon wedges.

prep + cook time 45 minutes **serves** 4
nutritional count per serving 34.6g total fat (6g saturated fat); 2510kJ (600 cal); 13g carbohydrate; 55g protein; 8g fibre

tip Leftover slaw will keep well for up to 2 days in the fridge.

Both prawns

and octopus provide good levels of the long chain omega-3 fats you might be taking as a fish oil supplement. These fats are crucially important in the brain and seem to play a role in cognitive function and brain health as we age. In children, these fats are essential for optimal brain development.

OMEGA-3

FATS ARE ANTI-INFLAMMATORY AND THEREFORE CAN BE HELPFUL IN RELIEVING ALL SORTS OF INFLAMMATORY CONDITIONS, INCLUDING ARTHRITIS, BUT MAY ALSO HELP TO REDUCE THE LOW-GRADE INFLAMMATION THAT OCCURS ALONGSIDE MANY CHRONIC DISEASES AND OBESITY.

prawns & octopus

Try throwing some octopus on your barbie for a change. 100g of cooked octopus has more than double the iron content of a similar amount of steak, but has 30% fewer kilojoules, hardly any fat and delivers a similar amount of protein. Octopus is also fabulously rich in vitamin B6, vitamin B12, phosphorus, copper and selenium.

For years people worried about the cholesterol found in prawns. However today we understand much more about what dietary factors affect our blood cholesterol profile. Dietary cholesterol is a minor factor. In fact in most of us the more cholesterol we eat the less our liver makes, and vice versa. If you have a poor cholesterol profile, concentrate on changing the types of fats in your diet rather than worrying about cholesterol in foods.

Octopus

has a green rating in Australia's Sustainable Seafood Guide, and while imported prawns are rated red due to grave concerns of fishing practices overseas, there are excellent Australian prawn fisheries with sustainable practice certifications.

Italian vincotto, literally meaning 'cooked wine', is a condiment made from boiling down grape must (skins, seeds and stems of grapes) until thick and syrupy. It is available from selected supermarkets and delis. You can use balsamic glaze instead.

baked sardines with fig and pine nut stuffing

⅔ cup (130g) chopped dried figs

⅓ cup (80ml) red wine vinegar

⅓ cup (80ml) olive oil

1 cup (70g) coarsely torn wholemeal sourdough breadcrumbs

1 medium red onion (170g), chopped finely

2 cloves garlic, crushed

2 teaspoons finely grated lemon rind

2 tablespoons chopped fresh rosemary

2 tablespoons chopped fresh flat-leaf parsley

2 tablespoons pine nuts, toasted

1 tablespoon lemon juice

12 sardines (660g), butterflied, with tails intact

2 tablespoons fresh rosemary leaves, extra

1 medium fennel bulb (300g), trimmed, sliced

1 medium radicchio (200g), cut into 12 wedges

2 tablespoons vincotto

1 Preheat oven to 200°C/400°F.
2 Combine fig and vinegar in a small saucepan over medium heat; simmer for 1 minute. Remove from heat; stand 10 minutes or until liquid is absorbed.
3 Meanwhile, heat 1 tablespoon of the oil in a large frying pan over medium heat; cook breadcrumbs, stirring, for 5 minutes or until golden. Remove from pan.
4 Heat another 1 tablespoon of the oil in same cleaned pan; cook onion, stirring, for 5 minutes or until soft. Add garlic, rind and rosemary; cook, stirring, for 1 minute or until fragrant. Remove pan from heat; stir in parsley, breadcrumbs, pine nuts, soaked figs and juice. Season to taste.
5 Place sardines, in a single layer, in a large oiled ovenproof dish. Place a heaped tablespoon of stuffing mixture inside each sardine cavity, fold sardines over slightly to enclose filling. Top with any remaining stuffing mixture and extra rosemary; drizzle with another 1 tablespoon of oil. Season. Bake for 15 minutes or until sardines are just cooked.
6 Meanwhile, brush fennel and radicchio with remaining oil; season. Cook fennel slices on a grill plate (or barbecue) over medium heat for 2 minutes each side or until charred lightly; transfer to a platter. Cook radicchio wedges on grill plate for 1 minute each side or until charred lightly and tender. Add radicchio to fennel; drizzle with half the vincotto.
7 Drizzle sardines with remaining vincotto. Serve with fennel and radicchio.

prep + cook time 1 hour **serves** 6
nutritional count per serving 24.2g total fat (4.3g saturated fat); 1722kJ (411 cal); 23.3g carbohydrate; 22.3g protein; 5.9g fibre

tip For the breadcrumbs, it's best to use day-old or stale bread.

mussels, kumara, chickpeas and greens in korma sauce

2 tablespoons olive oil

1 medium leek (350g), white part only, sliced

2 cloves garlic, crushed

⅓ cup (100g) korma paste

300g (9½ ounces) kumara (orange sweet potato), diced

270ml (9 fluid ounces) coconut milk

1 cup (250ml) fish stock

400g (12½ ounces) canned diced tomatoes

800g (1½ pounds) canned chickpeas (garbanzo beans), drained, rinsed

1kg (2 pounds) black mussels, scrubbed, bearded

250g (8 ounces) baby spinach

½ cup fresh coriander (cilantro) leaves

1 Heat oil in a large saucepan over medium-high heat; cook leek and garlic, stirring for 2 minutes or until softened.
2 Add korma paste to pan; cook, stirring, for 2 minutes. Add kumara, coconut milk, stock, tomatoes and chickpeas; bring to the boil. Reduce heat; simmer for 6 minutes or until kumara is tender. Stir in mussels; cook, covered, for 4 minutes or until mussels open. Stir in spinach until wilted.
3 Serve mussels scattered with coriander.

prep + cook time 35 minutes **serves** 4
nutritional count per serving 36.6g total fat (15.4g saturated fat); 2606kJ (623 cal); 41.9g carbohydrate; 25.5g protein; 12.8g fibre

serving suggestion Serve with steamed basmati rice.

This agrodolce (sweet and sour) Italian recipe uses currants and grapes for sweetness and vinegar for sourness. This traditional pairing of sour sweet as a sauce or flavouring is thought to have been brought to Sicily by the Arabs.

whiting with pine nuts, currants and tuscan cabbage

¼ cup (60ml) olive oil

1 medium red onion (150g), halved, sliced thinly

1 cup (170g) small red grapes, halved, if large

2 tablespoons currants

300g (9½ ounces) tuscan cabbage (cavalo nero), trimmed, chopped coarsely

¼ cup (60ml) red wine vinegar

⅓ cup (50g) pine nuts, toasted

1½ tablespoons olive oil, extra

8 sand whiting fillets (960g)

1 Heat olive oil in a large deep frying pan over medium-high heat; cook onion for 4 minutes or until softened. Add grapes and currants; cook, for 1 minute. Add cabbage and vinegar; cook tossing, for 1 minute or until cabbage is just wilted. Add pine nuts.
2 Heat extra oil in a large, frying pan over medium-high heat; cook fish, in two batches, for 1½ minutes each side or until just cooked through.
3 Serve fish on tuscan cabbage mixture.

prep + cook time 25 minutes **serves** 4
nutritional count per serving 30.5g total fat (4.1g saturated fat); 2027kJ (484 cal); 14.4g carbohydrate; 36.2g protein; 4.5g fibre

tip King George whiting is a delicately textured fish with a fine flake, and as is generally the case with small fish, it is a sustainable choice. You can use any other small white-fleshed fish such as snapper, bream, john dory or mirror dory.

ONE OF OUR CURRENT KEY ENVIRONMENTAL CONCERNS IS THE OVER FISHING OF OUR WATERS. FOR A NUTRITIONIST, IT IS SOMETHING OF A DILEMMA. FROM A NUTRITIONAL PERSPECTIVE THERE IS NO DOUBT OF THE ENORMOUS BENEFITS OF EATING MORE FISH, BUT FROM AN ENVIRONMENTAL PERSPECTIVE WE CANNOT CONTINUE TO TAKE MORE FISH THAN CAN REPOPULATE.

Fish are a valuable source of vitamin B12, only found in animal products, as well as small but useful amounts of iron and zinc.

White fish

is an excellent source of iodine. A 100g snapper fillet for example provides you with more than a quarter of your daily requirement. In Australia we no longer use so much iodised salt and so deficiency has re-emerged. Iodine is essential for the production of thyroid hormones that control metabolism. White fish also provide two minerals involved in many biological processed in the body including bone health – manganese and phosphorus. A serve of white fish can provide about a third of your daily manganese requirement and over three-quarters that for phosphorus.

small fish

While large oily fish often get all the nutritional kudos, small white fish are equally worthy of super food status. Although they don't contain the same high levels of omega-3 fats (with the exception of sardines), they do provide a wealth of other nutrients. They are protein rich with a 100g fillet providing you with about 20g of high quality protein (i.e. it contains all the essential amino acids we need), and with very little fat the kilojoule count is far lower.

One of the solutions to concerns of overfishing, is to take greater care with which fish we as consumers buy. We can learn which fish are at risk from overfishing and ensure we opt to buy from fisheries with sound sustainability practices in place. Of course when you choose from your local fishmonger you don't always have that information. So in this case, one factor to consider is the size of the fish.

Big fish

such as shark, swordfish and marlin take years to reach their size. Overfishing these large fish can have grave consequences. Furthermore these fish higher up the food chain are also those most likely to have accumulated levels of mercury that may be damaging to our health. By choosing smaller fish you have a win-win on both fronts.

Soba noodles are a low GI Japanese noodle made from a mixture of buckwheat and wheat, making them high in dietary fibre and a complete protein. Sodium content is high, however this is reduced significantly after cooking.

thai prawns with soba noodles and asparagus

200g (6½ ounces) green tea soba noodles

340g (11 ounces) thin asparagus, halved crossways

½ cup (80g) shelled frozen edamame (soybeans), thawed

1 cup fresh mint leaves

1 cup fresh thai basil leaves

16 uncooked large prawns (shrimp) (1.2kg), peeled, deveined, with tails intact

2 tablespoons olive oil

2 limes, cut into wedges

dressing

2 tablespoons finely grated palm sugar

⅓ cup (80ml) lime juice

¼ cup (60ml) fish sauce

2 fresh small red chillies, seeded, chopped finely

¼ cup (60ml) peanut oil

1 Make dressing.
2 Cook noodles in a saucepan of boiling water for 2 minutes or until almost tender. Add asparagus; cook a further 2 minutes or until noodles and asparagus are just tender. Drain, refresh under cold water; drain.
3 Place noodles and asparagus in a large bowl with edamame, herbs and dressing; toss gently to combine.
4 Combine prawns and oil in a medium bowl. Cook prawns on a heated grill plate (or grill or barbecue) for 1½ minutes each side or until just cooked through.
5 Serve noodle salad topped with prawns and lime wedges.
dressing Whisk ingredients together in a small bowl until sugar dissolves.

prep + cook time 25 minutes **serves** 4
nutritional count per serving 25.3g total fat (4.5g saturated fat); 2015kJ (481 cal); 22.1g carbohydrate; 22g protein; 6g fibre

tip Asparagus spears vary in thickness; if the ends are really thick, peel them from the bottom up to within 5cm (2 inches) of the tips.

For a light lunch you could probably get away with one small portion of fish. For heartier eaters, or as a main meal, you will want the quantity here.

bream with kohlrabi, watercress and walnut salad with buttermilk dressing

400g (12½ ounces) kohlrabi, trimmed, unpeeled
6 cups (180g) picked watercress sprigs
½ cup (55g) coarsely chopped roasted walnuts
2 green onions (scallions), sliced thinly
8 x 150g (4½-ounce) bream fillets
2 tablespoons olive oil

buttermilk dressing
1 tablespoon dijon mustard
1 tablespoon rice wine vinegar
¼ cup (60ml) olive oil
⅓ cup (80ml) buttermilk
⅓ cup fresh dill sprigs

1 Make buttermilk dressing.
2 Using a mandoline or V-slicer, slice kohlrabi into matchsticks (or grate coarsely). Place in a large bowl with watercress, nuts, onion and dressing; toss gently to combine.
3 Season fish on both sides. Heat oil in a large frying pan over high heat; cook fish, in two batches, for 1 minute each side or until just cooked through. Cover fish with foil, between batches, to keep warm.
4 Serve fish with kohlrabi salad.
buttermilk dressing Place ingredients in a screw-top jar; shake well. Season to taste. Refrigerate until needed.

prep + cook time 30 minutes **serves** 4
nutritional count per serving 48.3g total fat (9.9g saturated fat); 3059kJ (731 cal); 6.7g carbohydrate; 65.8g protein; 4.9g fibre

Butterflied sardines are boneless with the two fillets attached. To do this yourself, cut off the head just behind the gills. With a small knife, cut along the belly, from head to tail then open out. Holding the spine at head end, pull it down firmly towards the tail end and snip with scissors to release it.

grilled sardines with fennel and preserved lemon

2 teaspoons fennel seeds

½ teaspoon sea salt flakes

1 teaspoon freshly ground black pepper

12 butterflied sardines (540g)

⅓ cup (80ml) olive oil

2 tablespoons finely chopped preserved lemon rind

2 tablespoons lemon juice

150g (4½ ounces) baby green beans, trimmed

1 baby baby fennel (130g), trimmed

1 small lebanese cucumber (130g)

120g (4 ounces) radishes, sliced thinly

1 large avocado (350g), sliced

1 Using a mortar and pestle, crush fennel seeds with salt and pepper. Place sardines on a tray; sprinkle seed mixture on both sides. Cover with plastic wrap; refrigerate 20 minutes.
2 Meanwhile, place ¼ cup olive oil, preserved lemon rind and juice in a screw-top jar; shake well. Season to taste.
3 Cook beans in a saucepan of boiling salted water for 2 minutes or until just tender; drain. When cool enough to handle, cut beans in half lengthways.
4 Using a mandoline or V-slicer, cut fennel into very thin slices. Using a vegetable peeler, peel cucumber into ribbons.
5 Place beans, fennel, cucumber and radish in a large bowl with dressing; toss gently to combine.
6 Heat remaining oil in a large frying pan over medium-high heat; cook sardines for 1 minute each side or until just cooked through.
7 Layer salad and avocado on plates, top with sardines; serve immediately.

prep + cook time 35 minutes (+ refrigeration) **serves** 4
nutritional count per serving 41.5g total fat (8.4g saturated fat); 2073kJ (495 cal); 4.4g carbohydrate; 24.9g protein; 4.1g fibre

lean meats

Choosing the right meats can make a huge difference to your health and wellbeing, as well as that of the planet.

Sesame seeds contain a wonderful array of minerals. They are particularly rich in manganese and copper, and also provide significant levels of calcium, iron, magnesium, phosphorus and zinc. Tahini, a sesame seed spread, is a great way to give your body a sesame nutritional boost.

korean steak tacos with pickled vegetables

2 x 250g (8-ounce) grass-fed beef porterhouse steaks

4cm (1½-inch) piece fresh ginger (20g), grated

2 cloves garlic, crushed

2 tablespoons light soy sauce

½ teaspoon chilli flakes

1 medium carrot (120g), unpeeled, sliced thinly

1 lebanese cucumber (130g), sliced thinly

1 small red onion (100g), sliced thinly

1 clove garlic, extra, sliced

2 tablespoons rice wine vinegar

1 teaspoon caster (superfine) sugar

1 tablespoon vegetable oil

8 x 20cm (8-inch) wholegrain tortillas (320g)

1 butter (boston) lettuce (300g)

¼ cup (60ml) sweet chilli sauce

2 teaspoons sesame seeds, toasted

½ cup loosely packed fresh coriander (cilantro) leaves

1 Combine steaks, ginger, garlic, sauce and chilli flakes in a large bowl. Cover; stand for 15 minutes.
2 Meanwhile, combine carrot, cucumber, onion, extra garlic, vinegar and sugar in a large bowl. Cover; stand for 15 minutes.
3 Brush steaks on both sides with oil. Cook on heated grill plate (or barbecue) over high heat, for 2 minutes each side, for medium-rare or until cooked as desired. Remove from heat; cover with foil, rest for 5 minutes.
4 Place tortillas on heated grill plate for 30 seconds each side or until charred lightly.
5 Cut steak into thin slices. Top each tortilla with a few small lettuce leaves, sliced steak and pickled vegetables. Drizzle with chilli sauce. Top with sesame seeds and coriander.

prep + cook time 30 minutes (+ standing) **serves** 4
nutritional count per serving 27.8g total fat (9.3g saturated fat); 2418kJ (578 cal); 43.5g carbohydrate; 34g protein; 9g fibre

tip If tortillas are hard to separate, microwave in the opened bag (remove silica pack first) for 30 seconds.

The low-fat dieting era popularised chicken fillets, because the dark chicken meat near the bone has more fat. However, chicken cooked on the bone is tastier and the dark meat contains more nutrients, particularly iron and zinc. To enjoy every cut of the chicken, guilt-free, ditch the extra kilojoules in your diet by eliminating snack foods.

roast chicken with broad beans and lemon

1 medium lemon (140g)

3 cups (375g) fresh shelled broad (fava) beans

2 tablespoons olive oil

1.5kg (3 pounds) chicken pieces, bone-in, skin-on

4 green onions (scallions), cut into 4cm (1½-inch) lengths

4 cloves garlic, sliced thinly

8 sprigs fresh thyme

1½ cups (375ml) chicken stock

2 tablespoons lemon juice

½ cup loosely packed fresh mint leaves

2 tablespoons capers, rinsed

1 Preheat oven to 200°C/400°F.
2 Using a vegetable peeler, peel four 7cm (2¾-inch) strips of rind from the lemon. Squeeze juice from the lemon; you will need 2 tablespoons juice.
3 Cook broad beans in a saucepan of boiling water 2 minutes; drain. Refresh under cold running water; drain. Peel away skins then discard.
4 Heat oil in a large casserole dish over high heat; cook chicken pieces, in two batches, for 3 minutes each side or until browned. Remove from dish; drain excess fat from dish.
5 Add onion, garlic, thyme and rind strips to same dish; cook for 2 minutes. Return chicken and any juices to the dish with stock; bring to the boil. Transfer to the oven; cook, uncovered, for 40 minutes or until chicken is cooked through. Stir in broad beans; cook for a further 5 minutes or until heated through.
6 Serve chicken drizzled with lemon juice, topped with mint and capers.

prep + cook time 1 hour 15 minutes **serves** 4
nutritional count per serving 32.5g total fat (8.5g saturated fat); 2181kJ (521 cal); 5.9g carbohydrate; 47.3g protein; 9g fibre

tips You will need to buy about 1.7kg (3½ pounds) fresh broad beans in the pod to yield 3 cups, or you can use frozen broad beans. You can cook baby potatoes with the chicken. If you prefer, you can use a 1.5kg (3-pound) whole chicken chopped into pieces.

serving suggestion Serve with wholemeal couscous.

Kangaroo meat is lean and healthy. High in protein and iron and low in fat, kangaroo meat is a great alternative to more popular red meats. It is the ultimate free-range, organic meat containing no chemicals or antibiotics.

greek-style kangaroo bolognese

2 tablespoons olive oil
500g (1 pound) minced (ground) kangaroo
1 medium onion (150g), chopped finely
4 cloves garlic, crushed
4 sprigs fresh oregano
1 cup (250ml) red wine
800g (1½ pounds) canned diced tomatoes
2 cups (500ml) beef stock
1 teaspoon caster (superfine) sugar
400g (12½ ounces) wholemeal spaghetti
⅓ cup (50g) pitted kalamata olives, sliced
150g (4½ ounces) greek fetta, crumbled
¼ cup loosely packed fresh oregano leaves, extra
2 tablespoons olive oil, extra

1 Heat oil in a large, heavy-based saucepan over high heat; cook minced kangaroo, onion, garlic and oregano for 10 minutes or until browned, breaking up any lumps with a wooden spoon.
2 Add wine; cook for 1 minute. Add tomatoes, stock and sugar; bring to the boil. Reduce heat to medium; cook for 30 minutes or until sauce has reduced and thickened. Season to taste.
3 Meanwhile, cook spaghetti in a large saucepan of boiling, salted water for 12 minutes or until almost tender. Drain.
4 Add spaghetti to sauce; toss to combine. Serve topped with olives, fetta and extra oregano; drizzle with extra oil.

prep + cook time 50 minutes **serves** 4
nutritional count per serving 33.7g total fat (9.9g saturated fat); 3539kJ (845 cal); 70.6g carbohydrate; 49.9g protein; 14.1g fibre

tip You can use minced lamb instead of the minced kangaroo, if you like.

Quail is an excellent source of several of the B group vitamins, especially niacin with a single quail providing roughly half your daily requirement. Niacin plays a vital role in converting our food into energy and is essential for healthy skin and for nerves to function correctly.

char-grilled quail with cauliflower and pomegranate salad

1 small cauliflower (1kg), cut into 1.5cm (¾-inch) florets
2 tablespoons olive oil
6 medium quails (1kg), butterflied (see tip)
2 teaspoons ground coriander
1 teaspoon ground cinnamon
1 tablespoon fresh thyme leaves
2 tablespoons pomegranate molasses
2 lebanese cucumbers (260g), diced
1 medium red onion (170g), chopped finely
4 green onions (scallions), sliced thinly
1⅓ cups chopped fresh flat-leaf parsley
½ cup chopped fresh mint
1 medium pomegranate (320g), seeds removed
¼ cup (60ml) lemon juice
¼ cup (60ml) extra virgin olive oil
½ teaspoon honey

1 Preheat oven 220°C/425°F.
2 Divide cauliflower between two large oven trays; drizzle each tray with 2 teaspoons of the olive oil. Season. Bake for 15 minutes or until browned well.
3 Place quails on a large oven tray, sprinkle with spices, drizzle with remaining olive oil; season. Cook quails, skin-side down first, on a heated grill plate (or barbecue) over medium-high heat, for 3 minutes each side or until browned. Return quails to tray; top with thyme, drizzle with half the molasses. Bake for 8 minutes or until just cooked. Cover quail with foil; rest for 5 minutes.
4 Meanwhile, place cauliflower in a large bowl with cucumber, onions, herbs and half the pomegranate seeds. Whisk juice, extra virgin olive oil and honey in a small bowl. Pour dressing over salad; toss gently to combine.
5 Cut quails in half. Serve quail with cauliflower salad, drizzled with pan juices and remaining pomegranate molasses. Sprinkle with remaining pomegranate seeds.

prep + cook time 1 hour **serves** 4
nutritional count per serving 37.5g total fat (7.8g saturated fat); 2670kJ (645 cal); 23.6g carbohydrate; 47.3g protein; 13.2g fibre

tips To butterfly quails, cut down either side of the back bone with a pair of kitchen scissors, poultry shears or a knife; discard backbone, open quails out flat. To remove seeds from the pomegranate, cut a whole pomegranate in half and scrape the seeds from flesh with your fingers while holding the pomegranate upside down in a bowl of cold water; the seeds will sink and the white pith will float.

TODAY THE MEATS WE EAT THAT DOMINATE THE AUSTRALIAN DIET ARE BEEF, LAMB, CHICKEN AND PORK. DIVERSIFYING TO INCLUDE MORE GAME MEATS AND ALTERNATIVE POULTRY PROVIDES US WITH A NUTRITIONAL AND ENVIRONMENTAL BOOST.

Quail is produced in a free range environment. The meat provides high biological value protein, is reasonably low in fat and less than a third of that present is saturated fat. Quail is an excellent source of several of the B group vitamins, especially niacin. A single quail provides roughly half your daily requirement. Niacin plays a vital role in converting our food into energy, is essential for healthy skin and for nerves to function correctly.

quail & small chickens

From a sustainability and environmental perspective, there are advantages to us getting more of our protein from smaller, non-ruminant animals. Game birds and poultry fit this bill. If we look back through time and consider the foods our ancestors ate, thus the foods that have fuelled our evolution, smaller animals and birds would certainly have been hunted and been a regular part of our diet.

Small chickens

(aka spatchcock): these young chickens are specially prepared to make cooking easier. The smaller the bird the more fiddly it can be and so many producers make this easier for you by deboning, or removing the backbone to butterfly the bird. As with chicken there is more iron and zinc in the leg and thigh meat, so be sure to eat all parts of the bird. You'll benefit from a boost of B group vitamins, with niacin again being a star player.

Quail is a good source of many minerals including iron, zinc, selenium, phosphorus and copper.

warm beef salad with black-eyed peas, corn and chimichurri

You will need to start this recipe the day before as the black-eyed peas must be soaked overnight.

1 cup (200g) black-eyed peas
3 medium corn cobs (1.2kg), husks removed
2 tablespoons olive oil
3 x 200g (6½-ounce) sirloin steaks, trimmed
2 teaspoons ground cumin
2 teaspoons smoked paprika
1 medium red onion (170g), halved, sliced thinly
250g (8 ounces) heirloom tomatoes, halved
1 medium avocado (250g), chopped
2 fresh long red chillies, sliced thinly
½ cup fresh coriander (cilantro) leaves
2 tablespoons lime juice
2 tablespoons extra virgin olive oil

chimichurri

2 cloves garlic, crushed
1 cup coarsely chopped fresh flat-leaf parsley leaves
½ cup coarsely chopped fresh coriander (cilantro) leaves
1 teaspoon ground cumin
1 fresh small red chilli, chopped finely
½ cup (125ml) extra virgin olive oil
3 teaspoons lime juice

1 Place black-eyed peas in a medium bowl of cold water; soak overnight.
2 Drain black-eyed peas. Cook peas in a large saucepan of boiling water for 15 minutes or until tender; drain. Rinse under cold water; drain well.
3 Meanwhile, make chimichurri.
4 Brush corn with a little of the oil; season. Cook corn on a heated grill plate (or barbecue) over medium heat, turning occasionally, for 15 minutes or until charred and tender. Cool for 10 minutes. Cut kernels from cobs.
5 Brush steaks with a little of the oil, sprinkle with cumin and paprika; season. Cook steaks on heated grill plate over medium-high heat, for 3 minutes each side, depending on thickness, for medium rare or until cooked as desired. Remove from pan; cover with foil, rest for 5 minutes.
6 Place peas and corn kernels in a large bowl with onion, tomatoes, avocado, chilli, coriander, juice, extra virgin olive oil and a third of the chimichurri, season; toss gently to combine.
7 Serve salad topped with sliced steak and drizzled with remaining chimichurri.

chimichurri Process garlic, herbs, cumin, chilli and 1 tablespoon of the oil until roughly chopped. With motor operating, add remaining oil in a thin steady stream until smooth. Stir in juice. Season to taste.

prep + cook time 1 hour 5 minutes (+ standing) **serves** 4
nutritional count per serving 94.8g total fat (21.4g saturated fat); 5409kJ (1292 cal); 39.2g carbohydrate; 60.2g protein; 29g fibre

tip Chimichurri is a traditional Argentinian herb sauce served with grilled meats.

venison with baby beet salad and raspberry vinaigrette

You can use beef tenderloin instead of the venison if you like.

12 baby red beetroots (beets) (300g)
12 baby golden beetroots (beets) (300g)
⅓ cup (80ml) olive oil
1kg (2 pounds) venison tenderloin
12 shallots (400g)
100g (3 ounces) baby spinach
⅓ cup (50g) sunflower seeds, roasted
75g (2½ ounces) raspberries

raspberry vinaigrette
⅓ cup (80ml) raspberry vinegar
⅓ cup (80ml) olive oil
1 clove garlic, crushed
¼ cup fresh tarragon leaves
¼ cup fresh mint leaves
¼ cup fresh flat-leaf parsley leaves

1 Preheat oven to 180°C/350°F.
2 Trim beetroot; reserve 100g (3 ounces) of the nicest, smallest leaves. Wash all beetroot well. Place in a roasting pan; drizzle with half the oil. Cover with foil; roast for 30 minutes or until tender. Stand for 10 minutes. When cool enough to handle, remove skins (the skins should slip off easily, if not use a small knife). Cut beetroot in half.
3 Meanwhile, tie venison with kitchen string at 3cm (1¼-inch) intervals to form an even shape; season. Heat remaining oil over high heat in a large ovenproof frying pan; cook venison, turning, for 8 minutes or until browned all over. Add shallots; roast in the oven 20 minutes for medium-rare venison or until cooked as desired. Cover with foil; rest for 10 minutes. Cut venison into 1cm (½-inch) slices.
4 Make raspberry vinaigrette.
5 Place beetroot and reserved beetroot leaves in a large bowl with spinach, seeds and half the vinaigrette; toss to combine. Place salad on a platter; top with raspberries. Serve salad with venison; drizzle with remaining vinaigrette.
raspberry vinaigrette Place ingredients in a screw-top jar; shake well. Season to taste.

prep + cook time 1 hour **serves** 6
nutritional count per serving 33g total fat (5.7g saturated fat); 2440kJ (583 cal); 10g carbohydrate; 57.8g protein; 6.6g fibre

Turkey meat deserves to be embraced beyond festive eating as it is a very rich source of protein in relation to kilojoules, also all B vitamins are present in the meat, alongside iron and minerals. You can use chicken mince instead.

turkey koftas with fig and brown rice pilaf

You will need to soak 12 bamboo skewers in water for about 30 minutes before you start this recipe.

500g (1 pound) minced (ground) turkey

½ cup (35g) stale breadcrumbs

3 green onions (scallions), sliced thinly

2 cloves garlic, crushed

¼ teaspoon allspice

¼ teaspoon ground coriander

¼ teaspoon ground chilli

2 tablespoons olive oil

fig and brown rice pilaf

2 tablespoons olive oil

1 small onion (80g), chopped finely

2 cloves garlic, crushed

1 tablespoon finely grated orange rind

1 teaspoon ground cinnamon

½ teaspoon ground cumin

½ teaspoon ground coriander

500g (1 pound) packaged pre-cooked brown basmati rice

1 cup (250ml) chicken stock

⅓ cup (70g) chopped dried figs

100g (3 ounces) baby spinach leaves

1 Combine turkey, breadcrumbs, onion, garlic and spices in a large bowl. Roll 2 tablespoons of mixture into long oval shapes; you should have 12. Place koftas on a baking-paper-lined oven tray; refrigerate for 1 hour.
2 Make fig and brown rice pilaf.
3 Meanwhile, insert a skewer into each kofta; brush kofta well with oil. Cook kofta on heated grill plate (or grill or barbecue) on medium-high heat, turning occasionally, for 8 minutes or until cooked through.
4 Serve kofta with pilaf.
fig and brown rice pilaf Heat oil in a large saucepan over medium-high heat; cook onion and garlic, for 3 minutes or until soft. Stir in rind and spices; cook for 2 minutes. Add rice; stir to coat. Add stock; bring to the boil. Reduce heat to medium; cook, covered, for 8 minutes. Remove from heat; stir in figs and spinach. Season to taste.

prep + cook time 1 hour 20 minutes (+ refrigeration)
serves 4
nutritional count per serving 24.6g total fat (4.4g saturated fat); 2527kJ (604 cal); 57.9g carbohydrate; 34.2g protein; 6.9g fibre

serving suggestion Serve with yoghurt.

RED MEAT IS a fabulous source of high quality protein. Research has pretty conclusively shown that high protein diets help us to control our weight and most importantly keep any lost weight off. If you've been on the dieting merry-go-round think about how much red meat you consume. You might just find that including a little more helps you to control your appetite and as a result, eat less. (Note that doesn't mean low carbs – you can achieve a high protein diet while eating a moderate amount of quality carbs. In fact that is most likely to give you long term success.)

OUR SUPERFOODS ARE LEAN RED MEATS THAT ARE WILD OR PASTURE/GRASS FED WHERE POSSIBLE. GAME MEATS SUCH AS KANGAROO ARE ABOUT AS CLOSE AS WE CAN GET TO THE WILD MEAT OUR ANCESTORS WOULD HAVE CONSUMED. THEY ARE INCREDIBLY AND NATURALLY LEAN, WHILE BEING RICH IN NUTRIENTS AND A SOURCE OF OMEGA-3s. YOU MIGHT ALSO LIKE TO TRY VENISON IF YOU SPOT IT, BUT GRASS-FED BEEF AND LAMB ARE MOST WIDELY AVAILABLE AND WARRANT SUPERFOOD STATUS.

lean red meat

We can live without meat and we have every respect for those who are vegetarian... but there is no denying the nutritional benefits of good quality red meat. One of the most common nutrient deficiencies in the developed world is iron deficiency. In the extreme it results in anaemia, but even mild deficiencies cause an intolerance to cold, depressed immune function so more frequent coughs and colds, and an inability to exercise at your best. The trouble is, we're not very good at absorbing iron, particularly from plants. That's where red meat comes in. The haeme iron in meat is far better absorbed. Unfortunately it is women who need more iron, yet are the ones most likely to cut down on red meat.

If you're worried about the press there has been surrounding meat and colon cancer, be assured that the strongest evidence is for processed meats such as ham, bacon, salami and sausages. Fresh lean red meat is a totally different prospect. The other highly significant factor is that much of the epidemiological research on meat and chronic disease comes from the USA. In Australia, our agricultural systems for producing meat are far less intensive. We know that grass-fed meat is the best quality. It has higher levels of beneficial fats such as the omega-3s and lower overall levels of fat, especially long chain saturated fats. In Australia a majority of our animals are pasture fed for much of their lives. In the US the system is far more intensive and many animals never see grass. We cannot therefore consider all red meat in one nutritional basket.

RED MEAT is also rich in another mineral often low in typical diets – zinc. This is essential for immune function, hence you'll find it added to cold and flu remedies. Eating red meat a few times a week is all you need to significantly zinc-boost your diet.

white cooked chicken with ginger rice

1.4kg (2¾-pound) whole free-range chicken
3 green onions (scallions), sliced finely
6cm (2½-inch) piece fresh ginger (30g), cut into matchsticks
2 teaspoons sesame oil
2½ teaspoons caster (superfine) sugar
2 tablespoons peanut oil
¼ cup (60ml) light soy sauce
2 tablespoons oyster sauce
370g (12 ounces) gai lan, trimmed, chopped
1 fresh long red chilli, sliced thinly

white master stock
5 litres (20 cups) cold water
2½ cups (625ml) chinese rice wine (shao hsing)
8 green onions (scallions), trimmed, halved
10 cloves garlic, bruised
180g (5½ ounces) fresh ginger, sliced
2 tablespoons salt

ginger rice
2 cups (400g) jasmine rice
1 tablespoon vegetable oil
1 clove garlic, crushed
10cm (4-inch) piece fresh ginger (50g), sliced thinly

1 Make white master stock.
2 Remove excess fat from chicken cavity then rinse chicken. Carefully lower chicken, breast-side down, into simmering master stock, ensuring it is fully submerged. Poach chicken 30 minutes (there should be no more than the occasional ripple). Remove pan from heat; leave chicken in poaching liquid for 3 hours at room temperature to complete the cooking process. Using tongs, gently remove chicken from stock, being careful not to tear the breast. Place chicken on a tray; cool. Strain poaching liquid through a fine sieve; reserve poaching liquid.
3 Make ginger rice.
4 Place onion, ginger, half the sesame oil, ½ teaspoon of the sugar and 2 tablespoons of the reserved poaching liquid in a bowl. Heat peanut oil in a small frying pan until hot. Taking care, as mixture will split, pour hot oil over ginger mixture; reserve until ready to serve.
5 Place sauces, remaining sesame oil and remaining sugar in a screw-top jar; shake well. Cook gai lan in a large saucepan of boiling water for 2 minutes or until just tender; drain. Transfer gai lan to a serving bowl; add dressing and top with chilli.
6 Chop chicken into pieces and arrange on a platter; pour over reserved ginger mixture. Serve with ginger rice and gai lan.
white master stock Place ingredients in a large saucepan; bring to the boil. Reduce heat; simmer gently for 40 minutes.
ginger rice Rinse rice in a sieve under cold water until water runs clear. Heat oil in a large saucepan over medium heat; cook garlic and ginger 3 minutes. Add rice and 1 litre (4 cups) of the reserved poaching liquid; bring to the boil. Reduce heat to low; cook, covered, for 10 minutes or until most liquid is absorbed. Remove from heat; stand, covered, 10 minutes.

prep + cook time 4 hours 30 minutes
serves 6 as part of a banquet
nutritional count per serving 25.2g total fat (6.1g saturated fat); 2935kJ (701 cal); 63.5g carbohydrate; 31.9g protein; 3.3g fibre

sumac chilli lamb

1 large red onion (300g), cut into wedges

2 medium red capsicums (bell peppers) (400g), cut into strips

400g (12½ ounces) dutch (baby) carrots, trimmed, unpeeled

3 finger eggplants (480g), sliced lengthways

¼ cup (60ml) olive oil

860g (1¾ pounds) lamb backstraps, trimmed

1 tablespoon olive oil, extra

2 tablespoons sumac

1 teaspoon dried chilli flakes

100g (3 ounces) baby rocket (arugula)

¼ cup (60ml) lemon juice

2 tablespoons extra virgin olive oil

white bean puree

800g (1½ pounds) canned cannellini beans, drained, rinsed

1 clove garlic, crushed

¼ cup (60ml) lemon juice

⅓ cup (80ml) olive oil

1 Preheat oven to 180°C/350°F. Line a large roasting tray with baking paper.
2 Place vegetables on tray, drizzle with olive oil and season; toss to combine. Roast for 30 minutes or until tender.
3 Meanwhile, rub lamb with extra olive oil then roll in sumac and chilli. Cook lamb on heated grill plate (or barbecue) over medium-high heat, turning occasionally, for 4 minutes, for medium rare or until cooked to your liking. Cover with foil; rest for 5 minutes.
4 Meanwhile, make white bean puree.
5 Add rocket to vegetables, drizzle with juice and extra virgin olive oil; toss to combine. Spoon half the bean puree among plates, top with vegetable mixture. Cut lamb into thin slices; place on salad, drizzle with remaining bean puree.

white bean puree Process ingredients until smooth, adding a little water if necessary, until mixture reaches a dipping consistency. Season to taste.

prep + cook time 45 minutes **serves** 4
nutritional count per serving 63.3g total fat (12.2g saturated fat); 3910kJ (934 cal); 25.6g carbohydrate; 60g protein; 13.8g fibre

Although pork is perceived as being a fatty meat, a trimmed fillet is only about 2% fat. Pork breeding has changed in recent years making most pork these days pretty lean.

five spice pork fillet

2 shallots (50g), sliced thinly

2 cloves garlic, sliced thinly

4 corella pears (520g), each cut into 6 wedges

4cm (1½-inch) piece ginger (20g), cut into matchsticks

2 tablespoons brown sugar

2 tablespoons soy sauce

2 teaspoons chinese five-spice powder

¼ cup (60ml) olive oil

800g (1½ pounds) pork fillet, trimmed

2 tablespoons sesame seeds

100g (3 ounces) yellow beans

100g (3 ounces) baby green beans

1 Preheat oven to 180°C/350°F. Line a roasting tray with baking paper.
2 Place shallots, garlic, pears, ginger, sugar, sauce and five-spice in the tray, drizzle with 2 tablespoons of the oil; toss to combine. Roast for 20 minutes or until pears are just soft.
3 Meanwhile, rub pork with 2 teaspoons of the oil; roll in seeds. Heat remaining oil in an ovenproof frying pan over medium heat; cook pork until brown on all sides. Transfer pan to oven; roast pork for 12 minutes or just cooked through. Cover pork with foil; rest for 5 minutes.
4 Meanwhile, boil, steam or microwave beans for 3 minutes or until just tender; drain.
5 Serve sliced pork with roasted pear mixture, sauce and beans.

prep + cook time 40 minutes **serves** 4
nutritional count per serving 21.5g total fat (4.3g saturated fat); 2046kJ (489 cal); 19.6g carbohydrate; 47.3g protein; 8.2g fibre

Pork is STRICTLY SPEAKING A RED MEAT, HOWEVER NUTRITIONALLY IT'S PROFILE IS CLOSER TO WHITE MEAT. ALTHOUGH IT IS PERCEIVED AS BEING A FATTY MEAT, PORK BREEDING HAS CHANGED IN RECENT YEARS AND IN FACT MOST PORK TODAY IS PRETTY LEAN. AS WITH BIRDS, THE FAT IS SEPARABLE AND SO ONCE TRIMMED, PORK IS ONE OF THE LEANEST MEATS. A TRIMMED PORK FILLET IS ONLY ABOUT 2% FAT. PORK IS ALSO EXCEPTIONALLY RICH IN THIAMIN (VITAMIN B1) AND 100G OF RAW PORK FILLET, WHEN COOKED, PROVIDES 75% OF YOUR DAILY REQUIREMENT.

Pork is exceptionally rich in thiamin. Thiamin plays an essential role in metabolism, particularly of carbohydrates. Your requirement for thiamin is also increased if you drink alcohol.

white meats

White meats are essentially chicken and turkey, along with less commonly eaten birds and poultry. Nutritionally, these meats tend to be lower in kilojoules and fat then red meats, although there are exceptions. However, even in those birds with higher fat levels such as duck and goose, the fat is almost all in and just under the skin. This means that, unlike marbled fatty meats, you can remove most of the fat if you wish.

You don't really need to be so concerned about the fat on birds and poultry. The old days of trying to avoid all fat are long gone. We now know that it is processed fats in packaged foods and fast food that are most detrimental to us.

Some saturated fats are also known to worsen blood cholesterol profiles, may be harder to burn as fuel in the body and can have other negative effects at a cellular level. Monounsaturated fats, like those found in avocado and olive oil, seem to help reduce fat around your middle, be more readily burned as fuel and may also reduce the risk of several chronic diseases. Poultry, duck and other birds have a high percentage of these monounsaturated fats making them a healthier choice than fatty red meat cuts.

coconut, coriander chicken and vegetable curry

3 fresh long green chillies

1 large onion (200g), chopped

5cm (2-inch) piece fresh ginger (25g), chopped

4 cloves garlic, chopped

1 tablespoon ground coriander

1 tablespoon ground cumin

1 teaspoon salt

1kg (2 pounds) chicken thigh fillets

270ml (9 fluid ounces) canned coconut milk

2 cups (500ml) chicken stock

600g (1¼ pounds) kumara (orange sweet potato), unpeeled, cut into 2.5cm (1-inch) pieces

300g (9½ ounces) cauliflower, chopped

90g (3 ounces) baby spinach

1 tablespoon sesame seeds

⅓ cup (50g) roasted salted cashews

1 cup (280g) Greek-style yoghurt

½ cup coarsely chopped coriander (cilantro) leaves

¼ cup coarsely chopped fresh mint leaves

1 fresh long green chillies, chopped, extra

¼ cup lightly packed fresh coriander (cilantro) sprigs, extra

1 lime, cut into wedges

1 Remove seeds from two of the chillies; chop seeded chillies and one whole chilli.

2 To make curry paste, blend chopped chilli, onion, ginger, garlic, spices and salt until smooth.

3 Trim fat from chicken; cut chicken into 4cm (1½-inch) pieces. Heat 2 tablespoons of the coconut milk in a large saucepan over medium heat, add curry paste; cook, stirring, 3 minutes or until fragrant. Add chicken; cook, stirring, for 2 minutes or until combined. Add stock and remaining coconut milk; bring to the boil. Reduce heat; simmer, covered, for 10 minutes.

4 Add kumara to curry; simmer, covered, 5 minutes. Add cauliflower; simmer, covered, a further 5 minutes or until kumara and cauliflower are just tender. Stir in spinach until wilted.

5 Meanwhile, dry-fry seeds and nuts until browned lightly. Remove from pan; cool. Blend nut mixture until ground finely. Stir nut mixture into curry; stir in ¾ cup of the yoghurt and the chopped herbs. Season to taste.

6 Serve curry drizzled with remaining yoghurt, topped with extra chilli and extra coriander. Serve with lime wedges.

prep + cook time 50 minutes **serves** 6
nutritional count per serving 49g total fat (20g saturated fat); 3014kJ (720 cal); 30.8g carbohydrate; 36.2g protein; 7.4g fibre

tip Long chillies are usually mild but can vary in their heat intensity. Adjust the amount of chillies you use (or remove the seeds and membranes from all of them), according to your tolerance level.

serving suggestion Serve with steamed basmati or brown rice.

pork and fennel ragù with kumara and goat's cheese gnocchi

1.6kg (3¼-pound) piece boneless pork shoulder

2 tablespoons plain (all-purpose) spelt flour

1 tablespoon extra virgin olive oil

2 medium leeks (700g), white part only, sliced

2 trimmed celery stalks (200g), chopped

2 medium fennel bulbs (600g), fronds reserved, sliced thinly

4 cloves garlic, chopped

1 teaspoon chopped fresh thyme leaves

¼ teaspoon dried chilli flakes

2 cups (500ml) chicken stock

1 cup (250ml) water

1 cup (120g) whole marinated green sicilian olives

1 tablespoon lemon juice

kumara and goat's cheese gnocchi

1kg (2 pounds) kumara (orange sweet potato), unpeeled

120g (4 ounces) soft goat's cheese, crumbled

2 free-range egg yolks

1 cup (150g) plain (all-purpose) spelt flour, approximately

1 Remove rind and trim fat from pork. Cut pork into six pieces, toss in flour; shake away excess. Heat oil in a casserole dish over high heat; cook pork, in batches, for 10 minutes or until browned lightly. Remove from dish.
2 Cook leek, celery and fennel in same dish, stirring, over medium heat for 8 minutes or until softened. Add garlic, thyme and chilli; cook, stirring, 1 minute or until fragrant. Add stock and water; bring to the boil. Return pork to pan; stir to cover with liquid. Reduce heat to very low; simmer, covered, for 2 hours or until tender, stirring occasionally.
3 Meanwhile, make kumara and goat's cheese gnocchi.
4 Remove pork from pan; shred into smaller chunks. Return pork to pan with olives and juice. Season to taste. Cover; keep warm over low heat.
5 Cook gnocchi, in batches, in a large saucepan of boiling salted water for 2 minutes or until gnocchi float to the surface. Remove gnocchi with a slotted spoon; drain on paper towel.
6 Serve gnocchi topped with ragù, sprinkled with reserved fennel fronds and extra thyme leaves, if you like.
kumara and goat's cheese gnocchi Place whole kumara in a medium saucepan; cover with cold water. Cover; bring to the boil. Reduce heat; simmer, partially covered, for 45 minutes or until tender. Drain. Cool slightly; peel. Mash kumara in a large bowl until smooth. Cool to room temperature. Stir in cheese and egg yolks; season. Add enough of the flour to mix to a soft, slightly sticky dough. Divide mixture into six portions; roll each portion on a floured surface into a 2cm (¾-inch) thick log. Using a floured knife, cut logs into 2cm (¾-inch) lengths. Place gnocchi on a large plastic-wrap-lined tray in a single layer. Cover; refrigerate until required.

prep + cook time 2 hours 50 minutes **serves** 6
nutritional count per serving 12.7g total fat (4.8g saturated fat); 2499kJ (597 cal); 57.9g carbohydrate; 57.9g protein; 8.8g fibre

tips Prepare the ragù several hours or a day ahead; refrigerate until cold then skim any fat from the surface before reheating. You can use drained persian fetta instead of goat's cheese.

lamb wraps with red salad and harissa yoghurt

500g (1 pound) lamb backstraps

2 tablespoons harissa

2 tablespoons extra virgin olive oil

4 wholegrain barley wraps (180g)

¼ small red cabbage (200g), shredded finely

1 medium beetroot (beet) (170g), grated coarsely

½ medium red onion (85g), sliced thinly

4 radishes (60g), sliced thinly

1 tablespoon lemon juice

1 clove garlic, crushed

⅔ cup (190g) Greek-style yoghurt

⅓ cup loosely packed fresh coriander (cilantro) sprigs

⅓ cup loosely packed fresh mint sprigs

1 Preheat oven to 180°C/350°F.
2 Rub lamb with half the harissa; drizzle with half the oil. Season. Cook lamb on heated grill plate (or grill or barbecue) over medium-low heat, covered with a sheet of foil, for 4 minutes each side for medium or until done as desired. Remove lamb from heat; cover with foil, rest for 5 minutes.
3 Meanwhile, enclose barley wraps in foil; heat in oven 5 minutes.
4 For red salad, place cabbage, beetroot, onion and radish in a large bowl with juice, garlic and remaining oil; toss gently to combine. Season to taste.
5 Swirl remaining harissa through yoghurt.
6 Slice lamb thinly. Divide lamb, red salad, yoghurt mixture and herbs among wraps; roll up to serve.

prep + cook time 30 minutes **serves** 4
nutritional count per serving 21.5g total fat (6g saturated fat); 2064kJ (493 cal); 35.2g carbohydrate; 35.8g protein; 6.9g fibre

tip We used a milder harissa rather than the much hotter Tunisian one available in a tube. If using harissa in a tube, start with 1 teaspoon and add more to taste.

steak with cashew nam jim and asian greens

800g (1½ pounds) thick-cut rump steak

1 tablespoon peanut oil

350g (11 ounces) gai lan

270g (8½ ounces) baby buk choy, trimmed, quartered

100g (3 ounces) snow peas

4 green onions (scallions), sliced thinly

¼ cup (40g) unsalted roasted cashews, chopped coarsely

¼ cup loosely packed fresh coriander (cilantro) sprigs

cashew nam jim

2 shallots (50g), chopped

2 cloves garlic

3 fresh long green chillies, seeded, chopped

2 fresh coriander (cilantro) roots, chopped

2cm (¾-inch) piece fresh ginger (10g), chopped

2 tablespoons grated dark palm sugar

⅓ cup (50g) unsalted roasted cashews

⅓ cup (80ml) lime juice, approximately

1 tablespoon fish sauce, approximately

1 Make cashew nam jim.

2 Trim fat from steak; rub with oil, season. Cook steak on a heated grill plate (or grill or barbecue) on medium-high heat for 4 minutes each side for medium or until done as desired. Remove steak from heat; cover with foil, rest for 5 minutes.

3 Meanwhile, trim gai lan stalks; cut stalks from leaves. Steam stalks, in a single layer, in a large steamer over a wok or large suacepan of boiling water for 1 minute. Place separated buk choy on top; steam a further 2 minutes. Add snow peas and gai lan leaves; steam a further 2 minutes or until vegetables are just tender.

4 Place vegetables on a platter in layers, top with thickly sliced steak. Drizzle with steak resting juices, then top with cashew nam jim. Sprinkle with onion, nuts and coriander.

cashew nam jim Blend shallots, garlic, chilli, coriander root, ginger, sugar and cashews (or pound with a mortar and pestle) until mixture forms a paste. Transfer to a small bowl; stir in juice and fish sauce to taste.

prep + cook time 40 minutes **serves** 4
nutritional count per serving 35g total fat (9.7g saturated fat); 2888kJ (670 cal); 14g carbohydrate; 76.4g protein; 7.4g fibre

tips You will need about 3 limes for this recipe. Nam jim can be made a day ahead; keep tightly covered in the fridge until ready to use.

serving suggestion Serve with steamed jasmine or brown rice.

fruit & chocolate

We have an innate likeness for sweetness that is easy to exploit. But choose the right treats and you can not only enjoy them, you can give your health a boost at the same time.

Cherries are rich in vitamins and minerals as well as antioxidants. While fresh is best, if they are out of season, you can use frozen pitted cherries in this recipe instead.

apple, cherry and rosemary crumble

8 medium red apples (1.2kg)
¼ cup (60ml) water
3 cups (375g) cherries, pitted
1 teaspoon ground cinnamon
2 teaspoons vanilla extract
⅓ cup (80ml) pure maple syrup
1½ cups (240g) almonds
1 cup (160g) wholemeal self-raising flour
3 teaspoons fresh rosemary leaves, chopped finely
½ cup (120g) coconut oil, melted
2 tablespoons pure maple syrup, extra
1½ cups (420g) unsweetened vanilla-bean yoghurt

1 Preheat oven to 180°C/350°F.
2 Peel and core apples; cut into 2cm (¾-inch) pieces. Place apple and the water in a large saucepan; bring to the boil. Reduce heat to low; cook, covered, for 10 minutes or until apples are just tender.
3 Place apple and cooking liquid in a large bowl; stir in cherries, cinnamon, extract and maple syrup until combined. Spoon into a 2 litre (8-cup) shallow ovenproof dish.
4 Process nuts, flour and rosemary until nuts are chopped coarsely. With motor operating, add coconut oil and extra maple syrup until well combined. Spoon crumble mixture over fruit (piling crumble high on top of fruit as it will sink down during cooking).
5 Bake for 40 minutes or until crumble topping is golden and fruit is soft. Serve with yoghurt.

prep + cook time 1 hour **serves** 6
nutritional count per serving 45g total fat (21.5g saturated fat); 3169kJ (757 cal); 68.5g carbohydrate; 15.6g protein; 10.7g fibre

tip Coconut oil is a solidified oil sold in jars and is available from major supermarkets and health food stores. Melt coconut oil as you would butter, either in a small saucepan over low heat or in the microwave.

The winter months are citrus heaven for cooks. Swap navel oranges, for tangy tangelos (a cross between grapefruit and mandarin), large perfumed mandarins or ruby red grapefruit, or a mix of all of them.

orange and lemon yoghurt cups

1 vanilla bean

⅓ cup (75g) low GI caster (superfine) sugar (see tips)

½ cup (125ml) water

4 wide strips lemon rind

1 tablespoon lemon juice

2 blood oranges (360g), rind removed, sliced

2 medium oranges (480g), rind removed, sliced

3 cups (840g) Greek-style yoghurt

¼ cup loosely packed fresh mint leaves

1 Split vanilla bean in half lengthways; scrape seeds into a small saucepan. Add vanilla bean to pan with sugar, the water and rind; bring to the boil. Reduce heat; simmer for 6 minutes or until syrup has thickened slightly. Cool. Discard vanilla bean; stir in juice.
2 Combine orange slices and sugar syrup in a medium bowl.
3 Spoon yoghurt into four 1¼ cup (310ml) serving glasses; top with oranges, syrup and rind. Serve topped with mint.

prep + cook time 45 minutes **serves** 4
nutritional count per serving 12.7g total fat (8g saturated fat); 1756kJ (419 cal); 59.7g carbohydrate; 12.4g protein; 4.5g fibre

tips We used LoGiCane a low GI form of caster sugar. It is available from most major supermarkets. For lemon strips, use a vegetable peeler to peel wide strips and avoid taking off too much of the white pith with the rind as it is bitter. The syrup can be made 4 hours ahead and combined with the oranges; refrigerate until needed.

COCOA BEANS ARE FERMENTED, DRIED AND ROASTED, AND THE SHELL REMOVED TO PRODUCE CACAO NIBS. THESE ARE THEN GROUND AND THIS FORMS THE BASIS OF CHOCOLATE. USUALLY THE CACAO IS SEPARATED TO GIVE COCOA BUTTER AND COCOA SOLIDS AND YOU'LL FIND THESE LISTED AS INGREDIENTS ON THE PACK. SINCE THIS IS STILL A VERY BITTER TASTE, MOST CHOCOLATE IS SWEETENED AND MAY HAVE OTHER INGREDIENTS ADDED.

It's not just

your imagination. Chocolate really can cheer you up! The carbohydrates present raise levels of serotonin, the feel-good chemical in your brain, and chocolate contains a natural chemical called phenyl ethylamine that acts as a mood elevator.

Good quality

chocolate is not cholesterol raising and may even help to improve your overall cholesterol profile. Although cocoa butter is high in saturated fat, the main saturated fat present is stearic acid. This fat does not raise LDL-cholesterol, the so-called bad cholesterol. In fact studies have associated stearic acid with lower LDL-cholesterol. A good percentage of the other fats present are healthy monounsaturated fats, including oleic acid, the main fat in olive oil.

chocolate & cocoa

Several of the foods of ancient populations such as the Incas, Aztecs and Mayans are considered superfoods today and cocoa is one of them. Of course they didn't eat chocolate as we know it today, but they took the cacao bean and made it into a bitter tasting chocolate drink. Today chocolate is made far more delectable, but that also makes it easier to overeat.

Chocolate is

energy-dense meaning each bite contains a significant number of kilojoules. Devouring blocks of chocolate everyday will clearly not help your waistline. You're better off opting for dark chocolate with as high a cocoa content as possible (or that you can enjoy). This means you get the maximal amount of cocoa for antioxidant benefits, while limiting added sugar and the rich taste will mean you are satisfied with a small amount. Think quality over quantity.

One of the best ways to enjoy cocoa is by using pure cocoa powder (not to be confused with drinking chocolate powder). This ranks exceptionally high for antioxidant power, it's unexpectedly high in fibre, a good source of protein and has no added sugar or other undesirable additives. It also provides significant amounts of iron, magnesium, phosphorus, manganese and copper. You can add a tablespoon to milk along with a pinch of cinnamon and heat through to make a delicious chocolatey drink, or use in cooking and baking.

Unlike most chocolate mousse recipes, this one can be served the minute it is made. If you do wish to make it a day ahead, refrigerate, covered, then bring to room temperature before serving. You could also top each serving with cherries.

dark chocolate and ricotta mousse

⅓ cup (110g) rice malt syrup

1 tablespoon dutch-processed cocoa

2 tablespoons water

½ teaspoon vanilla extract

200g (6½ ounces) dark chocolate (70% cocoa), chopped

8 fresh dates (160g), pitted

½ cup (125ml) milk

2 cups (480g) ricotta

2 tablespoons pomegranate seeds

2 tablespoon chopped pistachios

1 Stir syrup, cocoa, the water and extract in a small saucepan over medium heat; bring to the boil. Remove from heat; cool.
2 Place chocolate in a small heatproof bowl over a small saucepan of simmering water (don't let the water touch the base of the bowl); stir until melted and smooth.
3 Process dates and milk until dates are finely chopped. Add ricotta; process until smooth. Add melted chocolate; process until well combined.
4 Spoon mousse into six ¾ cup (180ml) serving glasses. Spoon cocoa syrup on mousse; top with pomegranate seeds and nuts.

prep + cook time 20 minutes **serves** 6
nutritional count per serving 21g total fat (12g saturated fat); 2020kJ (482 cal); 62g carbohydrate; 12.3g protein; 3.8g fibre

tips Fresh pomegranate seeds can sometimes be found in the fridge section of supermarkets or good green grocers. If unavailable, cut a whole pomegranate in half and scrape the seeds from flesh with your fingers while holding the pomegranate upside down in a bowl of cold water; the seeds will sink and the white pith will float. Pomegranate seeds will keep refrigerated for up to a week.

citrus

One point
to note is that carotenoids, including beta-cryptoxanthin, are fat-soluble and therefore you need to have fat present to absorb them. You might like to ensure you eat some citrus at the end of a meal containing healthy fats, snack on them alongside a handful of nuts, or add them to salad with an extra virgin olive oil based dressing to get the full benefit.

Tangerines and oranges are one of the richest dietary sources of one of the carotenoid antioxidants called beta-cryptoxanthin. Some research studies have shown this to reduce the risk of lung and colon cancers, and may also reduce the risk of inflammatory disorders such as rheumatoid arthritis.

CITRUS FRUITS
include oranges, tangerines, mandarins, grapefruit varieties, clementine, cumquats, lemons and limes.

They are most famous for their vitamin C content – a single orange provides you with about 1.5 times your daily requirement. A good body of research suggests that optimal levels of vitamin C are somewhat higher than currently recommended. As a water-soluble nutrient, we cannot store it in the body and therefore need a vitamin C source in our diet every day for optimal health.

Grapefruit is rich in a flavonoid antioxidant called naringin. This plays a role in protecting the lungs from cellular damage caused by pollutants in the air and from cigarette smoke. Vitamin C is also important here making grapefruit a particularly good superfood for lung health. Naringin may also be involved in lowering the risk of colon cancer. Pink and red grapefruits get their colour from the carotenoids present, which may offer additional antioxidant benefits.

Try where
possible to eat some citrus fruit skin. It contains two antioxidants, limonene and coumarin, which have been shown to stimulate a detoxification enzyme that in turn helps rid the body of potentially carcinogenic compounds. Try adding some grated rind to your food, or gently stew lesser know citrus fruits such as cumquats, where you can, then eat the whole fruit including the skin.

There are two types of persimmons available in autumn: astringent and non-astringent. The first, is heart shaped and is eaten very ripe, otherwise the taste is very astringent. The other, which is sometimes sold as fuji fruit (fuji being the Japanese word for persimmon) is squat and eaten crisp.

honey and lime baked persimmons

You can use either astringent or non-astringent persimmons in this recipe. If you use the astringent variety, it is best to scrape away the flesh from the skin when eating.

4 persimmons (1kg), each cut into 6 wedges

1 lime, sliced thinly

4cm (1½-inch) piece fresh ginger (20g), sliced thinly

1½ tablespoons honey

200g (6½ ounces) passionfruit frozen yoghurt

1 tablespoon lime rind strips

1 Preheat oven to 200°C/400°F. Cut four 35cm (14-inch) pieces of baking paper.
2 Place pieces of paper lengthways in front of you then divide persimmon wedges among baking paper, placing them crossways in the centre. Top with lime slices and ginger; drizzle with honey. Bring short edges of paper together, fold over several times to secure, then tuck sides under to form a parcel. Place parcels on two oven trays.
3 Bake parcels for 15 minutes or until persimmon is soft. Serve opened parcels topped with spoonfuls of frozen yoghurt and lime rind.

prep + cook time 25 minutes **serves** 4
nutritional count per serving 3g total fat (1.7g saturated fat); 1197kJ (286 cal); 58g carbohydrate; 4g protein; 7.4g fibre

tip Use a zester to make the lime rind strips. If you don't have one, finely grate the rind instead.

spelt crêpes with poached pear and blueberries

2 free-range eggs

1 cup (250ml) milk

⅓ cup (50g) plain (all-purpose) spelt flour

⅓ cup (50g) wholemeal plain (all-purpose) spelt flour

360g (11½ ounces) ricotta

2 tablespoons pure maple syrup

1 teaspoon ground cinnamon

2 teaspoons coconut oil

poached pear and blueberries

½ cup (125ml) red wine

½ cup (125ml) freshly squeezed orange juice

1 cinnamon stick

2 tablespoons pure maple syrup

2 small corella pears (300g), unpeeled

125g (4 ounces) blueberries

1 Make poached pear and blueberries.
2 Meanwhile, process eggs, milk and flours until smooth. Transfer to a jug; stand for 20 minutes.
3 Whisk ricotta, maple syrup and cinnamon in a small bowl until smooth.
4 Brush a heated 20cm (8-inch) crêpe pan with a little of the coconut oil. Pour scant ¼ cups of batter into pan, swirling to coat the base; cook 30 seconds or until browned underneath. Turn crêpe; cook further 10 seconds or until browned lightly underneath. Transfer to a plate; cover to keep warm. Repeat with remaining oil and batter to make 8 crêpes in total.
5 Spread 2 tablespoons of the ricotta mixture on one quarter of each crêpe; fold crêpe into quarters over the filling. Serve crêpes with poached fruit and poaching liquid.
poached pear and blueberries Bring wine, juice, cinnamon and syrup to the boil in a medium saucepan over medium heat. Meanwhile, quarter and core pears; cut into thin wedges. Add pear to wine mixture; simmer, uncovered, 10 minutes or until tender. Add blueberries; remove from heat.

prep + cook time 35 minutes (+ standing) **serves** 4
nutritional count per serving 15g total fat (9g saturated fat); 1836kJ (438 cal); 52g carbohydrate; 17g protein; 6.8g fibre

tips The cooking time of the pear will depend on the ripeness. Buy ricotta fresh from the deli; it should be moist.

Buy fresh ricotta cut from a wheel from a deli or from the deli counter of a supermarket for the best texture. Pre-packaged ricotta will be too wet for this recipe. Cooling the cheesecake in the oven after it has been turned off, ensures that it will cool slowly and prevent the top from cracking.

ricotta and chocolate cheesecake with grapes

1 vanilla bean

750g (1½ pounds) ricotta

½ cup (175g) honey

2 tablespoons caster (superfine) sugar

2 teaspoons finely grated orange rind

3 free-range eggs

150g (4½ ounces) dark chocolate (70% cocoa), chopped finely

1 cup (160g) small red grapes

150g (4½ ounces) little bunches red grapes, extra

1 tablespoon honey, extra

1 Preheat the oven to 150°C/300°F. Grease a 22cm (9-inch) springform pan; line base and side with baking paper, extending the paper 3cm (1¼ inches) above the edge.
2 Split vanilla bean in half lengthways; scrape seeds into a large bowl of an electric mixer. Add ricotta, honey, sugar and rind to bowl; beat with an electric mixer on medium-high speed for 3 minutes or until smooth. Beat in eggs, one at time, until just combined. Stir in chocolate and half the grapes. Pour mixture into pan; top with remaining grapes.
3 Bake cheesecake for 55 minutes or until the centre is almost firm to touch. Cool in the oven with the door ajar. Refrigerate cheesecake for 4 hours or until firm.
4 Just before serving, top cheesecake with extra grapes; drizzle with extra honey.

prep + cook time 1 hour 30 minutes (+ cooling & refrigeration)
serves 12
nutritional count per serving 10g total fat (5.7g saturated fat); 993kJ (237 cal); 30.4g carbohydrate; 7.8g protein; 0.4g fibre

tip When chopping the chocolate aim for fairly even pieces about 5mm (¼-inch) in size.

Berries are high in vitamin C and contain many potentially beneficial plant chemicals that have been shown to have anti-cancer, anti-viral and anti-bacterial properties.

Pomegranate is an ancient fruit that remains popular in Mediterranean, Middle-Eastern and Indian diets. In these areas pomegranate has long been used medicinally, but recent research is uncovering many factors about the fruit that may well account for some very real health benefits. Pomegranate is one of the highest ranking fruits for antioxidant power and it is particularly rich in a group of polyphenols called ellagitannins. This can bind cancer-causing molecules rendering them inactive, and has been shown to have an anti-cancer effect on several cancers including breast, skin, prostate and colon.

berries

The beautiful array of blues, reds and purples of berries are indicative of the antioxidants present. The colour comes from the anthocyanins present. These are part of the flavonoid family of antioxidants. Studies show a high intake of anthocyanins from berries to have a beneficial effect on cardiovascular health and on reducing cancer risk.

While exotic berries such as goji and acai may well have good antioxidant power, there are in fact fantastic benefits from fresh and frozen local berries. Choose from whatever is available near you. Raspberries, blackberries, blueberries, strawberries and blackcurrants all have varying levels of different beneficial plant chemicals and are worthy of daily inclusion in your diet.

Studies suggest that pomegranates can improve insulin sensitivity and help to control blood glucose levels, assist in improving blood cholesterol profiles and exert an anti-inflammatory effect. All up, it really is worth the effort of removing the seeds. Pomegranate works equally well in savoury and sweet dishes. Try adding it to your salads, in a marinade for roast meat or sprinkle it over your muesli.

Rich in antioxidants, strawberries are a great source of vitamin C and fibre. They are also a good source of the trace mineral manganese which is essential for healthy bone structure.

lemon cakes with roasted strawberries

⅔ cup (110g) almonds

⅔ cup (100g) wholemeal plain (all-purpose) spelt flour

2 free-range eggs

⅓ cup (75g) low GI caster (superfine) sugar (see tip)

¼ cup (90g) rice malt syrup

3 teaspoons finely grated lemon rind

2 tablespoons extra virgin olive oil

2 tablespoons lemon juice

½ teaspoon baking powder

roasted strawberries

500g (1 pound) strawberries, halved

¼ cup (90g) honey

1½ tablespoons lemon juice

1 Preheat oven to 180°C/350°F. Grease an 8-hole (½-cup/125ml) loaf pan tray. Line base of pan holes with strips of baking paper, extending the paper 3cm (1¼ inches) over long sides.
2 Process nuts and 2 teaspoons of the flour until finely ground.
3 Beat eggs, sugar, syrup and rind in a small bowl with an electric mixer on medium-high speed for 10 minutes or until thick and pale. Reduce speed to low, gradually beat in oil and juice until just combined. Stir in nut mixture, then sifted remaining flour and baking powder; return any husks to bowl. Spoon mixture into holes.
4 Bake cakes for 25 minutes or until a skewer inserted in the centre comes out clean. Stand cakes in pans for 5 minutes, before turning top-side up onto a wire rack to cool.
5 Make roasted strawberries.
6 Serve cakes warm with roasted strawberries.
roasted strawberries Combine ingredients in a medium ovenproof dish. Roast, uncovered, for 10 minutes or until softened. Stir gently. Stand 5 minutes.

prep + cook time 1 hour (+ standing) **makes** 8
nutritional count per cake 13.8g total fat (1.6g saturated fat); 1280kJ (306 cal); 37.7g carbohydrate; 7g protein; 3.5g fibre

tip We used LoGiCane, a low GI form of caster sugar. It is available from most major supermarkets.

serving suggestion Serve with Greek-style yoghurt.

Parfait means 'pefect' in French and there's a lot about this dessert that's perfect. For starters, it's easy to make and doesn't melt too quickly which means it's great for entertaining. It's also packed with valuable antioxidant-rich berries.

chocolate, honey and red berry parfait

You will need to start this recipe a day ahead.

½ cup (80g) almonds

1 vanilla bean

400g (12½ ounces) ricotta

⅔ cup (230g) honey

2 cups (560g) Greek-style yoghurt

100g (3 ounces) dark chocolate (70% cocoa), chopped

100g (3 ounces) raspberries

100g (3 ounces) cherries, halved, pitted

2 tablespoons honey, extra

1 Preheat oven to 180°C/350°F. Line the base of a 10.5cm x 23.5cm (4-inch x 9½-inch) terrine or loaf pan with baking paper, extending the paper over two long sides.
2 Spread nuts in a single layer on an oven tray. Roast nuts for 10 minutes or until skins begin to split. Cool. Chop nuts coarsely.
3 Meanwhile, split vanilla bean lengthways; scrape seeds into a food processor. Add ricotta and honey; process until smooth. Transfer mixture to a large bowl.
4 Fold in chopped nuts, yoghurt, chocolate, raspberries and cherries. Spoon mixture into pan; smooth top. Cover with foil. Freeze for 8 hours or overnight until firm.
5 Wipe base and sides of pan with a warm cloth. Turn parfait onto a chopping board; cut into slices. Divide slices among shallow serving dishes. Stand for 10 minutes before serving, drizzled with extra honey.

prep + cook time 40 minutes (+ cooling, freezing & standing)
serves 8
nutritional count per serving 19g total fat (8.8g saturated fat); 1743kJ (416 cal); 50g carbohydrate; 12g protein; 2g fibre

tip Cut the parfait with a large straight-bladed knife.

serving suggestion Serve with extra raspberries and cherries.

glossary

allspice also known as pimento or jamaican pepper; so-named because it tastes like a combination of nutmeg, cumin, clove and cinnamon. Available whole or ground.

almonds flat, pointy-tipped creamy white kernel with a brown skin.
blanched brown skins removed.
flaked paper-thin slices.

baking paper also called parchment paper or baking parchment – is a silicone-coated paper that is primarily used for lining baking pans and oven trays so cooked food doesn't stick, making removal easy.

barley a nutritious grain used in soups and stews. Hulled barley, the least processed, is high in fibre. Pearl barley has had the husk removed then been steamed and polished so that only the "pearl" of the original grain remains, much the same as white rice.

bay leaves aromatic leaves from the bay tree available fresh or dried; adds a strong, slightly peppery flavour.

beans
borlotti also called roman beans or pink beans, can be eaten fresh or dried. Interchangeable with pinto beans due to their similarity in appearance – pale pink or beige with dark red streaks.
broad (fava) also called windsor and horse beans; available dried, fresh, canned and frozen. Fresh should be peeled twice (discarding the outer long green pod and the beige-green tough inner shell); frozen beans have had their pods removed but the beige shell still needs removal.
cannellini a small white bean similar in appearance and flavour to other white beans (great northern, navy or haricot), all of which can be substituted for the other. Available dried or canned.
kidney medium-sized red bean, slightly floury in texture, yet sweet in flavour.
white a generic term we use for canned or cannellini, haricot, navy or great northern beans belonging to the same family, *phaseolus vulgaris*.

beetroot (beets) also known as red beets; firm, round root vegetable.

bicarbonate of soda (baking soda) a raising agent.

breadcrumbs
fresh bread, usually white, processed into crumbs.
panko (japanese) are available in two kinds: larger pieces and fine crumbs; have a lighter texture than Western-style ones. Available from Asian food stores and most supermarkets.
stale made by grating, blending or processing 1- or 2-day-old bread.

broccolini a cross between broccoli and chinese kale; long asparagus-like stems with a long loose floret, both completely edible. Resembles broccoli but is milder and sweeter in taste.

buk choy also known as bok choy, pak choi, chinese white cabbage or chinese chard; has a fresh, mild mustard taste. Use both stems and leaves. Baby buk choy, also known as pak kat farang or shanghai bok choy, is smaller and more tender than buk choy.

butter use salted or unsalted (sweet) butter; 125g is equal to one stick of butter (4 ounces).

buttermilk originally the term given to the slightly sour liquid left after butter was churned from cream, today it is made from no-fat or low-fat milk to which specific bacterial cultures have neen added. Despite its name, it is actually low in fat.

capers grey-green buds of a warm climate shrub (usually Mediterranean); sold dried and salted or pickled in a vinegar brine. Rinse before using.

capsicum (bell pepper) also called pepper. Comes in many colours: red, green, yellow, orange and purplish-black. Be sure to discard seeds and membranes before use.

cardamom a spice native to India and used extensively in its cuisine; can be purchased in pod, seed or ground form. Has a distinctive aromatic, sweetly rich flavour.

celeriac (celery root) tuberous root with knobbly brown skin, white flesh and a celery-like flavour. Keep peeled celeriac in acidulated water to stop it discolouring. It can be grated and eaten raw in salads; used in soups and stews; boiled and mashed like potatoes; or sliced thinly and deep-fried as chips.

cheese
fetta Greek in origin; a crumbly textured goat- or sheep-milk cheese having a sharp, salty taste. Ripened and stored in salted whey.
fetta, persian a soft, creamy fetta marinated in a blend of olive oil, garlic, herbs and spices. It is available from most larger supermarkets.
goat's made from goat's milk, has an earthy, strong taste; available in both soft and firm textures, in various shapes and sizes, and sometimes rolled in ash or herbs.
haloumi a firm, cream-coloured sheep-milk cheese matured in brine; haloumi can be grilled or fried, briefly, without breaking down. Should be eaten while still warm as it becomes tough and rubbery on cooling.
parmesan also called parmigiano; is a hard, grainy cow-milk cheese originating in Italy. Reggiano is the best variety.
pecorino the Italian generic name for cheeses made from sheep's milk; hard, white to pale-yellow cheeses. If you can't find it, use parmesan.
ricotta a soft, sweet, moist, white cow-milk cheese with a low fat content and a slightly grainy texture. The name roughly translates as "cooked again" and refers to ricotta's manufacture from a whey that is itself a by-product of other cheese making.

chickpeas (garbanzo beans) an irregularly round, sandy-coloured legume. Firm texture even after cooking, a floury mouth-feel and robust nutty flavour; available canned or dried (reconstitute for several hours in cold water before use).

chilli use rubber gloves when seeding and chopping fresh chillies as they can burn your skin. Removing membranes and seeds lessens the heat level.
long available both fresh and dried; a generic term used for any moderately hot, thin, long (6-8cm/2¼-3¼ inch) chilli.

chinese cooking wine (shao hsing) also known as chinese rice wine; made from fermented rice, wheat, sugar and salt with a 13.5% alcohol content. Inexpensive and found in Asian food shops; if you can't find it, replace with mirin or sherry.

chinese five-spice powder a fragrant mixture of ground cinnamon, cloves, star anise, sichuan pepper and fennel seeds.

choy sum also known as pakaukeo or flowering cabbage, a member of the buk choy family; easy to identify with its long stems, light green leaves and yellow flowers. Stems and leaves are edible.

cinnamon available in sticks (quills) and ground into powder; used as a sweet, fragrant flavouring in sweet and savoury foods.

cocoa powder also known as cocoa; dried, unsweetened, roasted and ground cocoa beans (cacao seeds).
dutch-processed is treated with an alkali to neutralise its acids. It has a reddish-brown colour, a mild flavour and easily dissolves in liquids.

coconut
flaked dried flaked coconut flesh.
milk not the liquid found inside the fruit (coconut water), but the diluted liquid from the second pressing of the white flesh of a mature coconut (the first pressing produces coconut cream).

coriander (cilantro) also known as pak chee or chinese parsley; a bright-green leafy herb with a pungent flavour. Both the stems and roots of coriander are also used in cooking; wash well before using. Also available ground or as seeds; these should not be substituted for fresh coriander as the tastes are completely different.

couscous a fine, grain-like cereal product made from semolina; it swells to three or four times its original size when liquid is added.

cumin also known as zeera or comino; has a spicy, nutty flavour.

dukkah an Egyptian specialty spice mixture made up of roasted nuts, seeds and an array of aromatic spices.

edamame (shelled soy beans) available frozen from Asian food stores and some supermarkets.

eggplant also known as aubergine. Ranging in size from tiny to very large and in colour from pale green to deep purple.

fennel also known as finocchio or anise; a white to very pale green-white, firm, crisp, roundish vegetable about 8-12cm in diameter. The bulb has a slightly sweet, anise flavour but the leaves have a much stronger taste. Also the name given to dried seeds having a licorice flavour.

fish sauce called naam pla (Thai) and nuoc naam (Vietnamese); the two are almost identical. Made from pulverised salted fermented fish (often anchovies); has a pungent smell and strong taste. Available in varying degrees of intensity, so use according to your taste.

flour
chickpea (besan) made from ground chickpeas so is gluten-free and high in protein. Used in Indian cooking.
plain (all-purpose) an all-purpose wheat flour.
self-raising plain flour sifted with baking powder in the proportion of 1 cup flour to 2 teaspoons baking powder.
wholemeal also known as wholewheat flour; milled with the wheat germ so is higher in fibre and more nutritional than plain flour.

gai lan also known as chinese broccoli, gai larn, kanah, gai lum and chinese kale; appreciated more for its stems than its coarse leaves.

ginger, pickled pink or red in colour, paper-thin shavings of ginger pickled in a mixture of vinegar, sugar and natural colouring. Available from Asian food shops.

kaffir lime leaves also known as bai magrood. Aromatic leaves of a citrus tree; two glossy dark green leaves joined end to end, forming a rounded hourglass shape. A strip of fresh lime peel may be substituted for each kaffir lime leaf.

kecap manis a thick soy sauce with added sugar and spices. The sweetness is derived from the addition of molasses or palm sugar.

kumara (orange sweet potato) the Polynesian name of an orange-fleshed sweet potato often confused with yam.

labne is a soft cheese made by salting plain (natural) yoghurt and draining it of whey for up to 2 days until it becomes thick enough to roll into small balls, which may be scattered with or rolled in chopped herbs or spices.

leeks a member of the onion family, the leek resembles a green onion but is much larger and more subtle in flavour. Tender baby or pencil leeks can be eaten whole with minimal cooking but adult leeks are usually trimmed of most of the green tops then chopped or sliced.

lentils (red, brown, yellow) dried pulses often identified by and named after their colour; also known as dhal.
French-style green are a local cousin to the famous French lentils du puy; green-blue, tiny lentils with a nutty, earthy flavour and a hardy nature that allows them to be rapidly cooked without disintegrating.

maple syrup, pure distilled from the sap of sugar maple trees found only in Canada and the USA. Maple-flavoured syrup or pancake syrup is not an adequate substitute for the real thing.

miso fermented soybean paste. There are many types of miso, each with its own aroma, flavour, colour and texture; it can be kept, airtight, for up to a year in the fridge. Generally, the darker the miso, the saltier the taste and denser the texture. Salt-reduced miso is available. Buy in tubs or plastic packs.

mushrooms
enoki clumps of long, spaghetti-like stems with tiny, snowy white caps.
flat large, flat mushrooms with a rich earthy flavour. They are sometimes misnamed field mushrooms, which are wild mushrooms.
oyster also known as abalone; grey-white mushroom shaped like a fan. Prized for their smooth texture and subtle, oyster-like flavour.
shiitake when fresh are also called chinese black, forest or golden oak mushrooms; although cultivated, they are large and meaty and have the earthiness and taste of wild mushrooms. When dried, they are called donko or dried chinese mushrooms; rehydrate before use.
swiss brown also known as cremini or roman mushrooms, are light brown mushrooms having a full-bodied flavour.

muslin inexpensive, undyed, finely woven cotton fabric called for in cooking to strain stocks and sauces; if unavailable, use disposable coffee filter papers.

mustard seeds are available in black, brown or yellow varieties. They are available from major supermarkets and health-food shops.

noodles, soba thin, pale-brown noodle originally from Japan; made from buckwheat and varying proportions of wheat flour. Available dried and fresh and flavoured.

oil
cooking spray we use a cholesterol-free spray made from canola oil.
olive made from ripened olives. Extra virgin and virgin are the first and second press, respectively, of the olives and are therefore considered the best; the "extra light" or "light" name on other types refers to taste not fat levels.
peanut pressed from ground peanuts; has a high smoke point (capacity to handle high heat without burning).
sesame made from roasted, crushed, white sesame seeds; used as a flavouring rather than a cooking medium.

onions
green (scallions) also known as, incorrectly, shallot; an immature onion picked before the bulb has formed. Has a long, bright-green edible stalk.
red also known as spanish, red spanish or bermuda onion; a sweet-flavoured, large, purple-red onion.
shallots also called french shallots, golden shallots or eschalots; small, brown-skinned, elongated members of the onion family.

pepitas (pumpkin seeds) are the pale green kernels of dried pumpkin seeds; they can be bought plain or salted.

pine nuts not a nut but a small, cream-coloured kernel from pine cones. They are best roasted before use to bring out the flavour.

pomegranate dark-red, leathery-skinned fresh fruit about the size of an orange filled with hundreds of seeds, each wrapped in an edible lucent-crimson pulp having a unique tangy sweet-sour flavour.

pomegranate molasses not to be confused with pomegranate syrup or grenadine; pomegranate molasses is thicker, browner and more concentrated in flavour – tart, sharp, slightly sweet and fruity. Available from Middle Eastern food stores or specialty food shops.

quinoa pronounced keen-wa; is a gluten-free grain. It has a delicate, slightly nutty taste and chewy texture.

radicchio a red-leafed Italian chicory with a refreshing bitter taste that's eaten raw and grilled. Comes in varieties named after their places of origin, such as round-headed verona or long-headed treviso.

rice
basmati a white, fragrant long-grained rice. Wash several times before cooking.
jasmine fragrant long-grained rice; white rice can be substituted, but will not taste the same.

roasting/toasting nuts and dried coconut can be roasted in the oven to restore their fresh flavour and release their aromatic essential oils. Spread them evenly onto an oven tray then roast at 180°C/350°F for about 5 minutes. Desiccated coconut, pine nuts and sesame seeds roast more evenly if stirred over low heat in a heavy-based frying pan; their natural oils will help turn them golden brown.

saffron available ground or in strands; imparts a yellow-orange colour to food once infused. The quality can vary greatly; the best is the most expensive spice in the world.

silver beet also known as swiss chard; mistakenly called spinach.

snow peas also called mange tout (eat all). Snow pea tendrils, the growing shoots of the plant, are also available at greengrocers.
sprouts are the tender new growths of snow peas.

soy sauce made from fermented soya beans. Several variations are available in most supermarkets and Asian food stores. We use japanese soy sauce unless otherwise indicated.

spinach also known as english spinach and, incorrectly, silver beet. Baby spinach leaves are best eaten raw in salads; the larger leaves should be added last to soups, stews and stir-fries, and should be cooked until barely wilted.

sugar
brown very soft, finely granulated sugar retaining molasses for its characteristic colour and flavour.
caster (superfine) finely granulated table sugar.

palm also called nam tan pip, jaggery, jawa or gula melaka; made from the sap of the sugar palm tree. Light brown to black in colour and usually sold in rock-hard cakes; use with brown sugar if unavailable.

sumac a purple-red, astringent spice ground from berries growing on shrubs that flourish wild around the mediterranean; adds a tart, lemony flavour to food. Available from spice shops and major supermarkets.

tahini a rich, sesame-seed paste, used in most Middle-Eastern cuisines, especially Lebanese, in dips and sauces.

tamarind the tamarind tree produces clusters of hairy brown pods, each of which is filled with seeds and a viscous pulp, that are dried and pressed into the blocks of tamarind found in Asian food shops. Gives a sweet-sour, slightly astringent taste to marinades, sauces and dressings.

tomato
canned whole peeled tomatoes in natural juices; available crushed, chopped or diced. Use undrained.
paste triple-concentrated tomato puree used to flavour soups, stews and sauces.
truss small vine-ripened tomatoes with vine still attached.

turmeric also called kamin; is a rhizome related to galangal and ginger. Must be grated or pounded to release its acrid aroma and pungent flavour. Known for the golden colour it imparts, fresh turmeric can be substituted with the more commonly found dried powder.

vanilla
bean dried, long, thin pod from a tropical golden orchid; the minuscule black seeds inside the bean impart a luscious flavour.
extract obtained from vanilla beans infused in water; a non-alcoholic version of essence.

vinegar
balsamic originally from Modena, Italy, there are now many balsamic vinegars on the market ranging in pungency and quality depending on how, and for how long, they have been aged. Quality can be determined up to a point by price; use the most expensive sparingly.
white balsamic is a clear and lighter version of balsamic vinegar; it has a fresh, sweet, clean taste.

water chestnut resembles a chestnut in appearance, hence the English name. They are small brown tubers with a crisp, white, nutty-tasting flesh. Their crunchy texture is best experienced fresh, however, canned water chestnuts are more easily obtained.

watercress one of the cress family, a large group of peppery greens. Highly perishable, so must be used as soon as possible after purchase.

wombok (napa cabbage) also known as peking cabbage, chinese cabbage or petsai; elongated in shape with pale green, crinkly leaves.

wrappers, gow gee made of flour, egg and water, are found in the refrigerated or freezer section of Asian food stores and supermarkets. These come in different thicknesses and shapes. Thin wrappers work best in soups, while the thicker ones are best for frying.

yeast (dried and fresh), a raising agent used in dough making. Granular (7g sachets) and fresh compressed (20g blocks) yeast can almost always be substituted for the other.

yoghurt, Greek-style plain yoghurt strained in a cloth (traditionally muslin) to remove the whey and to give it a creamy consistency.

conversion chart

measures

One Australian metric measuring cup holds approximately 250ml; one Australian metric tablespoon holds 20ml; one Australian metric teaspoon holds 5ml. The difference between one country's measuring cups and another's is within a two- or three-teaspoon variance, and will not affect your cooking results. North America, New Zealand and the United Kingdom use a 15ml tablespoon.

All cup and spoon measurements are level. The most accurate way of measuring dry ingredients is to weigh them. When measuring liquids, use a clear glass or plastic jug with the metric markings.

The imperial measurements used in these recipes are approximate only. Measurements for cake pans are approximate only. Using same-shaped cake pans of a similar size should not affect the outcome of your baking. We measure the inside top of the cake pan to determine sizes.

We use large eggs with an average weight of 60g.

dry measures

metric	imperial
15g	½oz
30g	1oz
60g	2oz
90g	3oz
125g	4oz (¼lb)
155g	5oz
185g	6oz
220g	7oz
250g	8oz (½lb)
280g	9oz
315g	10oz
345g	11oz
375g	12oz (¾lb)
410g	13oz
440g	14oz
470g	15oz
500g	16oz (1lb)
750g	24oz (1½lb)
1kg	32oz (2lb)

liquid measures

metric	imperial
30ml	1 fluid oz
60ml	2 fluid oz
100ml	3 fluid oz
125ml	4 fluid oz
150ml	5 fluid oz
190ml	6 fluid oz
250ml	8 fluid oz
300ml	10 fluid oz
500ml	16 fluid oz
600ml	20 fluid oz
1000ml (1 litre)	1¾ pints

length measures

metric	imperial
3mm	⅛in
6mm	¼in
1cm	½in
2cm	¾in
2.5cm	1in
5cm	2in
6cm	2½in
8cm	3in
10cm	4in
13cm	5in
15cm	6in
18cm	7in
20cm	8in
22cm	9in
25cm	10in
28cm	11in
30cm	12in (1ft)

oven temperatures

The oven temperatures in this book are for conventional ovens; if you have a fan-forced oven, decrease the temperature by 10-20 degrees.

	°C (CELSIUS)	°F (FAHRENHEIT)
Very slow	120	250
Slow	150	300
Moderately slow	160	325
Moderate	180	350
Moderately hot	200	400
Hot	220	425
Very hot	240	475

index

A
alliums 123
almonds 61
    miso almond vegie patties 42
    pasta with almond and walnut paste, pears and broad beans 74
apple, cherry and rosemary crumble 213
avocado 103
    chilled avocado soup with crab 116
    kidney bean, onion and rocket frittatas with avocado dressing 16
    pesto with prawns and pasta 119

B
beef
    korean steak tacos with pickled vegetables 177
    steak with cashew nam jim and asian greens 209
    warm beef salad with black-eyed peas, corn and chimichurri 186
    wombok and herb salad with beef and tamarind dressing 96
beetroot
    roast beetroot, garlic and chia seed tart 135
    venison with baby beet salad and raspberry vinaigrette 189
berries 229
    chocolate, honey and red berry parfait 233
    lemon cakes with roasted strawberries 230
    poached pear and blueberries 225
brassicas 115
bread, seeded pumpkin 54
bream with kohlrabi, watercress and walnut salad with buttermilk dressing 171
broad beans
    pasta with almond and walnut paste, pears and broad beans 74
    prawn, pea and broad bean frittata with lemon herb salad 152
    roast chicken with broad beans and lemon 178
broccoli and ocean trout salad 132

C
cabbage
    pickled cabbage salad 42

(*cabbage* continued)
    seeded carrot and cabbage fillo pie 128
    whiting with pine nuts, currants and tuscan cabbage 164
    wombok and herb salad with beef and tamarind dressing 96
capsicum 131
    spelt pasta with braised capsicum, nuts and chilli 69
cashews 61
    coconut-roasted pumpkin and cauliflower with chilli, lime and, 88
    nam jim 209
cauliflower
    cauliflower and tomato gratin 124
    char-grilled quail with cauliflower and pomegranate salad 182
    coconut-roasted pumpkin and cauliflower with chilli, lime and cashews 88
    spiced chickpea and cauliflower dosa 46
chicken 201
    coconut, coriander chicken and vegetable curry 202
    roast with broad beans and lemon 178
    small chickens (spatchcock) 185
    white cooked, with ginger rice 194
chickpeas
    chickpea, barley, orange and cherry salad 53
    mussels, kumara, chickpeas and greens in korma sauce 163
    roast kumara and pear salad with crunchy chickpeas 84
    spiced chickpea and cauliflower dosa 46
    vegetable harira soup 57
chilli 131
    coconut-roasted pumpkin and cauliflower with chilli, lime and cashews 88
    spelt pasta with braised capsicum, nuts and chilli 69
    sumac chilli lamb 197
chocolate 217
    chocolate, honey and red berry parfait 233
    dark chocolate and ricotta mousse 218
    ricotta and chocolate cheesecake with grapes 226
citrus fruits 221
clams 151 *see also* seafood
cocoa 217
coconut, coriander chicken and vegetable curry 202
coconut-roasted pumpkin and cauliflower with chilli, lime and cashews 88

curry
    coconut, coriander chicken and vegetable 202
    kumara, eggplant and coconut 120

D
dairy food 19 *see also* yoghurt
dressing 32, 88, 132, 168, 189
    buttermilk 171
    creamy zucchini 79
    spicy 80
    tamarind 96
dumplings, spinach and ginger 80

E
eggplant
    kumara, eggplant and coconut curry 120
    romesco sauce with eggplant and zucchini 58
eggs 27
    fried eggs and spiced yoghurt sauce 11
    huevos rancheros 28
    kidney bean, onion and rocket frittatas with avocado dressing 16
    mushroom, tomato and goat's cheese omelettes 31
    poached eggs, flat mushrooms and spinach with kumara rösti 12
    prawn, pea and broad bean frittata with lemon herb salad 152
    soft-boiled egg and brown rice nasi goreng 20

F
fennel
    grilled sardines with fennel and preserved lemon 172
    pea, fennel and spinach lasagne 107
    pork and fennel ragù with kumara and goat's cheese gnocchi 205
fish 167 *see also* seafood
five spice pork fillet 198
freekeh 73
    spiced freekeh with cucumber and garlic minted yoghurt 65
french toast with poached cherries 24
frittata/s
    kidney bean, onion and rocket, with avocado dressing 16
    prawn, pea and broad bean frittata with lemon herb salad 152

G

gai lan, sichuan 100
garlic 123
grains 73 *see also* rice
    chickpea, barley, orange and cherry salad 53
    french toast with poached cherries 24
    mediterranean grain salad with honey cumin labne 70
    muesli with poached pears and sheep's milk yoghurt 62
    rosemary and tomato barley risotto with mozzarella 45
    seeded pumpkin bread 54
    spelt crêpes with poached pear and blueberries 225
    spelt pasta with braised capsicum, nuts and chilli 69
    spelt pizza with kumara, pepitas and goat's cheese 66
    spelt spaghetti with cherry tomato sauce and vongole 111
    spiced freekeh with cucumber and garlic minted yoghurt 65
greek-style kangaroo bolognese 181

H

harissa and tomato prawns with fetta 144
honey and lime baked persimmons 222
huevos rancheros 28

K

kale 83
    salad with creamy zucchini dressing 79
kangaroo bolognese, greek-style 181
kidney bean, onion and rocket frittatas with avocado dressing 16
kumara
    kumara and goat's cheese gnocchi 205
    kumara, eggplant and coconut curry 120
    mussels, kumara, chickpeas and greens in korma sauce 163
    poached eggs, flat mushrooms and spinach with kumara rösti 12
    roast kumara and pear salad with crunchy chickpeas 84
    spelt pizza with kumara, pepitas and goat's cheese 66

L

labne 32
    labne and tomato salad with seeds 32
    mediterranean grain salad with honey cumin labne 70
lamb
    spicy roast pumpkin with 127
    sumac chilli 197

(*lamb* continued)
    wraps with red salad and harissa yoghurt 206
lasagne, pea, fennel and spinach 107
leafy greens 83
lean red meat 193
lemon cakes with roasted strawberries 230
lime and cardamom sheep's milk yoghurt with tropical fruit 15

M

mediterranean grain salad with honey cumin labne 70
miso almond vegie patties 42
mousse, dark chocolate and ricotta 218
muesli with poached pears and sheep's milk yoghurt 62
mushrooms
    mushroom, tomato and goat's cheese omelettes 31
    poached eggs, flat mushrooms and spinach with kumara rösti 12
mussels 151
    mussels, kumara, chickpeas and greens in korma sauce 163

N

nuts 61
    cashew nam jim 209
    coconut-roasted pumpkin and cauliflower with chilli, lime and cashews 88
    miso almond vegie patties 42
    pasta with almond and walnut paste, pears and broad beans 74
    romesco sauce with eggplant and zucchini 58
    spelt pasta with braised capsicum, nuts and chilli 69
    winter vegetable sauté with prosciutto and hazelnuts 92

O

octopus 159
oils 103
omelettes, mushroom, tomato and goat's cheese 31
orange and lemon yoghurt cups 214
oysters 151
    cucumber and shallot salad, with 147

P

pasta
    almond and walnut paste, pears and broad beans, with 74
    pea, fennel and spinach lasagne 107
    pesto with prawns and 119
    spelt spaghetti with cherry tomato sauce and vongole 111

(*pasta* continued)
    spelt, with braised capsicum, nuts and chilli 69
    spinach and broccolini pasta with rocket and walnut pesto 95
pea, fennel and spinach lasagne 107
pepitas 49
    pumpkin seed pesto 139
    spelt pizza with kumara, pepitas and goat's cheese 66
persimmons, honey and lime baked 222
pizza, spelt, with kumara, pepitas and goat's cheese 66
pork 201
    five spice pork fillet 198
    pork and fennel ragù with kumara and goat's cheese gnocchi 205
poultry 201
prawns 159
    harissa and tomato prawns with fetta 144
    prawn, pea and broad bean frittata with lemon herb salad 152
    thai prawns with soba noodles and asparagus 168
pulses 41
    chickpea, barley, orange and cherry salad 53
    kidney bean, onion and rocket frittatas with avocado dressing 16
    mussels, kumara, chickpeas and greens in korma sauce 163
    roasted tomato and white bean soup 112
    spiced chickpea and cauliflower dosa 46
    spicy white bean panzanella 38
    vegetable harira soup 57
    warm beef salad with black-eyed peas, corn and chimichurri 186
    white bean puree 197
pumpkin
    coconut-roasted pumpkin and cauliflower with chilli, lime and cashews 88
    seeded pumpkin bread 54
    spicy roast pumpkin with lamb 127
    stir-fried pumpkin, water spinach and tomatoes with five spice 108

Q

quail 185
    char-grilled with cauliflower and pomegranate salad 182
quinoa 49
    indian-spiced quinoa cakes with tomatoes 50
    salad with haloumi and pomegranate 37

R

red meat, lean 193

rice
  ginger 194
  fig and brown rice pilaf 190
  seared wasabi salmon and brown rice salad 140
  silver beet 'risotto' 99
  soft-boiled egg and brown rice nasi goreng 20
ricotta and chocolate cheesecake with grapes 226
ricotta, baked, with char-grilled vegetables and salsa verde 23
romesco sauce with eggplant and zucchini 58
rosemary and tomato barley risotto with mozzarella 45

S

salad
  bream with kohlrabi, watercress and walnut salad with buttermilk dressing 171
  broccoli and ocean trout 132
  char-grilled quail with cauliflower and pomegranate 182
  chickpea, barley, orange and cherry salad 53
  kale salad with creamy zucchini dressing 79
  labne and tomato salad with seeds 32
  mediterranean grain salad with honey cumin labne 70
  quinoa salad with haloumi and pomegranate 37
  roast kumara and pear salad with crunchy chickpeas 84
  seared wasabi salmon and brown rice 140
  spicy white bean panzanella 38
  vegetable larb 104
  venison with baby beet salad and raspberry vinaigrette 189
  warm beef salad with black-eyed peas, corn and chimichurri 186
  wombok and herb salad with beef and tamarind dressing 96
salmon 143
  baked salmon fillets with tahini sauce and tabbouleh 148
  salmon and zucchini burgers with green hummus 155
  seared wasabi salmon and brown rice salad 140
seafood 143 see also mussels; prawns; salmon
  baked baby barramundi with pumpkin seed pesto 139
  baked sardines with fig and pine nut stuffing 160
  bream with kohlrabi, watercress and walnut salad with buttermilk dressing 171

(seafood continued)
  broccoli and ocean trout salad 132
  chilled avocado soup with crab 116
  grilled sardines with fennel and preserved lemon 172
  harissa and tomato prawns with fetta 144
  oysters with cucumber and shallot salad 147
  small fish 167
  snapper and bay leaf skewers with root vegetable slaw 156
  spelt spaghetti with cherry tomato sauce and vongole 111
  whiting with pine nuts, currants and tuscan cabbage 164
seeds 49
  indian-spiced quinoa cakes with tomatoes 50
  labne and tomato salad with seeds 32
  muesli with poached pears and sheep's milk yoghurt 62
  quinoa salad with haloumi and pomegranate 37
  roast beetroot, garlic and chia seed tart 135
  seeded carrot and cabbage fillo pie 128
  seeded pumpkin bread 54
shellfish 151
sichuan gai lan 100
silver beet 'risotto' 99
snapper and bay leaf skewers with root vegetable slaw 156
soup
  chilled avocado soup with crab 116
  roasted tomato and white bean 112
  vegetable harira 57
spatchcock (small chickens) 185
spelt crêpes with poached pear and blueberries 225
spelt pasta with braised capsicum, nuts and chilli 69
spelt pizza with kumara, pepitas and goat's cheese 66
spelt spaghetti with cherry tomato sauce and vongole 111
spiced chickpea and cauliflower dosa 46
spiced freekeh with cucumber and garlic minted yoghurt 65
spicy white bean panzanella 38
spinach 83
  pea, fennel and spinach lasagne 107
  poached eggs, flat mushrooms and spinach with kumara rösti 12
  spinach and broccolini pasta with rocket and walnut pesto 95
  spinach and ginger dumplings 80
steak see beef
stir-fried pumpkin, water spinach and tomatoes with five spice 108
sumac chilli lamb 197

T

tomato
  cauliflower and tomato gratin 124
  labne and tomato salad with seeds 32
  mushroom, tomato and goat's cheese omelettes 31
  roasted tomato and white bean soup 112
  rosemary and barley risotto with mozzarella 45
  stir-fried pumpkin, water spinach and tomatoes with five spice 108
turkey koftas with fig and brown rice pilaf 190

V

vegetable harira soup 57
vegetable larb 104
vegetable, tofu and noodle broth, japanese-style 87
venison with baby beet salad and raspberry vinaigrette 189

W

walnuts 61
  pasta with almond and walnut paste, pears and broad beans 74
white meats 201
whiting with pine nuts, currants and tuscan cabbage 164
winter vegetable sauté with prosciutto and hazelnuts 92
wombok and herb salad with beef and tamarind dressing 96

Y

yoghurt 19
  cucumber yoghurt 46
  fried eggs and spiced yoghurt sauce 11
  garlic minted yoghurt 65
  lamb wraps with red salad and harissa yoghurt 206
  lime and cardamom sheep's milk yoghurt with tropical fruit 15
  muesli with poached pears and sheep's milk yoghurt 62
  orange and lemon yoghurt cups 214

Z

zucchini
  creamy zucchini dressing 79
  romesco sauce with eggplant and zucchini 58
  salmon and zucchini burgers with green hummus 155